The British Folk Scene

Popular Music in Britain

The British Folk Scene

Musical Performance and Social Identity

Niall MacKinnon

Open University Press
Buckingham · Philadelphia

Open University Press
Celtic Court
22 Ballmoor
Buckingham
MK18 1XW

and

1900 Frost Road, Suite 101
Bristol, PA 19007, USA

First Published 1993

A catalogue record of this book is available from the British Library

ISBN 0 335 09773 1 (pb)   0 335 09774 X (hb)

Library of Congress Cataloging-in-Publication Data
MacKinnon, Niall.
    The British folk scene: musical performance and social identity/Niall MacKinnon.
        p.   cm. – (Popular music in Britain)
    Includes bibliographical references and index.
    ISBN 0-335-09774-X. – ISBN 0-335-09773-1 (pbk.)
    1. Folk music – Social aspects – Great Britain.   2. Popular music – Social aspects
– Great Britain.   3. Music and society.   I. Series.
ML3650.M3   1993
781.62′62′00904 – dc20   93-4036
                                                                            CIP
                                                                            MN

Typeset by Best-set Typesetter Ltd., Hong Kong
Printed in Great Britain by St Edmundsbury Press Ltd,
Bury St Edmunds, Suffolk

Contents

Fetishized as a commodity, music is illustrative of the evolution of our entire society: deritualize a social form, repress an activity of the body, specialize its practice, generalize its consumption, then see to it that it is stockpiled until it loses all meaning. Today, music heralds ... the establishment of a society of repetition in which nothing will happen any more. But at the same time, it heralds the emergence of a formidable subversion.

Jacques Attali (1985: 5–11)

Editorial Preface

What *is* British popular music? Does such a thing exist? What makes certain music and songs popular? And who made the musical cultures of these islands? What did Scots, Welsh, Irish and North American people have to do with the process? What part did people in the English regions play – the Geordies, Cockneys, Midlanders and all the rest? Where did the Empire fit in? How did European 'high' culture affect what most people played and sang? And how did all these factors vary in significance over time? In the end, just how much do we know about the history of musical culture on these tiny patches of land? The truth is that we know very little, and this realisation led to this series.

The history of British people and culture has been dominated by capitalism for centuries; and capitalism helped polarise people into classes not only economically, but culturally too. Music was never *simply* music: songs were never *simply* songs. Both were produced and used by particular people in particular historical periods for particular reasons, and we have recognised this in the way in which we have put this series together.

Every book in this series aims to exemplify and to foster inter-disciplinary research. Each volume studies not only 'texts' and performances, but institutions and technology as well, and the culture practices and sets of social relationships through which music and songs were produced, disseminated and consumed. Ideas, values, attitudes and what is generally referred to as ideology are taken into account, as are factors such as gender, age, geography and traditions. Nor is our series above the struggle. We do not pretend to have helped produce an objective record. We are, unrepentantly, on the side of the majority, and our main perspective is from 'below', even though the whole musical field needs to be in view. We hope that by clarifying the history of popular musical culture we can help clear the ground for a genuinely democratic musical culture of the future.

Dave Harker and Richard Middleton

Acknowledgements

I would like to thank my wife, Janice MacKinnon, and my children, for their support, encouragement and forbearance. I gratefully acknowledge the assistance of the Economic and Social Research Council (ESRC), award no. A428424172, which funded a studentship enabling me to undertake the research on which this book is based. I would like to record my appreciation for the guidance and encouragement of my supervisor, Michael Hepworth. I thank Elizabeth Mickleburgh, Ken MacKinnon and Janice MacKinnon who undertook proofreading at very short notice. The series editors, Dave Harker and Richard Middleton, provided many useful comments and criticisms of earlier drafts of this book. Finally, I would like to give thanks to the numerous individuals who answered my questions and did so much to make the fieldwork a pleasure.

Introduction

The aim of this book is to seek to understand a musical genre, the contemporary British folk scene, in terms of identifying the social factors that give it coherence. The 'folk scene' or 'folk revival', which are the two terms by which it is popularly known, comprises the folk club and folk festival movement which arose in Britain in the late 1950s and continues to the present day.

I use the term 'musical genre' in this book to refer to a musical form in conjunction with the social grouping with which it is associated. The English language does not have a single word to encapsulate this meaning and I have selected 'genre' in preference to other alternatives such as 'form', 'sub-culture' or 'scene' which have other drawbacks. This book examines the predeterminants of musical events within the genre, focusing upon the construction and meaning of performance, staging and sound, and the association of these with social identity. The book focuses upon the interpretation of musical performance as social action, a shift of focus away from understanding music as sound towards thinking of it as behaviour. Such a perspective offers additional insights to understanding musical thought and musical action, to understanding the social in music. A dominant theme is that the performance of music is dependent upon a whole range of musical, paramusical and non-musical actions from which and through which it derives meaning.

The central questions posed are: Is the main appeal of folk music in Britain today a certain organisation of musical sound, or is it something beyond this? If so, what is this 'something' and how does it relate to the nature of the musical event? Is the music doing something other for its audience than simply providing musical enjoyment? Is the link with the past which is affirmed in the notion of revival an aspect which audiences directly relate to and identify with?

Music engenders a feeling of fear among many of my colleagues in social research, I suspect due to the centrality of musical literacy in formal musical education. Being a musician, albeit an untrained one playing solely for a hobby, I had overcome this apprehension. I was no more afraid of tackling this project than enroling for a course in poetry without prior understanding of phonetics or the physical properties of sound waves. I mention this because what started off as a resistance to becoming embroiled in detailed musicological interpretations of musical pieces led me in a specific research direction. This was to search for order, pattern and consistency within a musical genre, from which I hoped to start unravelling a sociological understanding.

I did not want to be overly drawn into musicology. My aim was not to dissect musical syntax but to investigate human behaviour. But neither did I want the music to disappear. I wanted to understand the music as humanly organised sound but my central research task was not to investigate sound. I thus undertook a number of distinct research tasks which included a historical examination of the folk scene concentrating upon the way in which different ideologies were expressed, an in-depth survey of folk club audiences, interviews with performers and those involved in organising folk music events, and a qualitative study of folk music performances.

Throughout the study I interviewed a wide range of relevant insiders: musicians, attenders, organisers, promoters, presenters, agents, entrepreneurs and so on. The themes dealt with included the following: patterns of entry into folk music to identify paths of socialisation; the transition to playing as a professional or semi-professional performer; the forms of musical learning folk musicians underwent; the careers of folk musicians; how they organised their performance; how tours were structured; financial arrangements; and the criteria for achieving 'success'.

I was particularly interested in the following points of comparison with other musical genres: how musicians thought about and constructed their performing repertoires; their relationships with their audience; whether musicians liked playing in formal or informal settings; how they categorised their material; what made for a good or bad musical performance; the kinds of crisis and problem which occurred.

The term 'folk music' used by the genre itself derives from a conceptualisation of this music by the adherents as a revival of what was thought to be the native traditional music transmitted through what was seen as an oral folk process. But folk music, in the sense of the music to be found on the folk scene, is more than that, and indeed is something different. The genre is generally referred to by the adherents as the 'folk scene' or the folk 'revival'. These are all terms used within the genre, and in this book it is in these senses – as labels – that I use the terms 'folk' and 'folk scene' except where otherwise stated. But the notions of 'folk', 'tradition' and 'revival' are important organising concepts and as terms have a far wider currency than they are used in 'the folk revival'. They are ideological terms. How the folk scene articulates with the past and how it has utilised these concepts will form a central component of this study.

But before moving on to an account of the genre I will first examine how we may seek to understand and study the social in music.

1   *The Social in Music*

This work arose in part from a feeling of dissatisfaction. Music is still relegated to the sidelines within the social sciences. Despite the major significance of music within Western society and some excellent sociological writing on music in the last decade, a consideration of music rarely forms a component of sociology teaching. Until the last ten years there were few serious attempts in British academia to grasp the import and significance of popular music.

But with the launching of the journal *Popular Music* in 1981, and the founding of the International Association for the Study of Popular Music in 1983, a number of music writers, researchers, academics, fans and enthusiasts have founded what is in essence a new discipline. It has brought together the methods of the social sciences and musicology in such a way that the music itself is no longer a secondary, but a primary focus of social scientific studies of musical behaviour. The meaning of the music of rock 'n' roll, punk, country and western, and so on is now being investigated by social scientific researchers as well as musicological ones. The significance of using interpretations of musical action as a tool to understand society has a longer tradition within anthropology, which spawned the sub-discipline of ethnomusicology, but this, until relatively recently, was chiefly concerned with the study of non-Western cultures. A major reason may be that music has come to occupy a specialised and prestigious place within academia, utilising a very particular range of skills and methods. This discourages social scientists from opening a dialogue because of a lack of specialist musical training and a perceived lack of the requisite conceptual tools.

However, millions of people manage to listen to records without musical training. Many millions more throughout the world sing or play a musical instrument without being able to read written notation, and all these people 'get something' out of what they do. It is true that an understanding of musical syntax, in the specialised sense of being able to isolate specific sonic relationships in order to articulate the grammar of musical sound, may assist an understanding of what it is that performers or listeners (or dancers, worshippers, etc.) are 'getting out' of a given performance, but it is also the case that the overuse of highly technical terms can obscure and block a wider discourse.

My intention is not to spell out the necessary terms of a dialogue between sociology and musicology (and, heaven forbid, university music departments and sociology departments). What I wish to unravel are the means by which social science may relate to music, and to the social relationships involved in the production of music; in other words, to a sociological understanding of musical performance, reception and consumption. In this introductory chapter I wish to trace how various writers, some social scientists, some not, some musicians and some not, have come to understand the meaning of music; not necessarily what a 'composer' means by a given 'composition', but what a musical performance means to those who partake in it; what they mean by what they do, how they define what they do and how we might bring the methods of sociological enquiry to offer a distinctly sociological interpretation.

The term 'music' carries many connotations. It can be thought of as certain configurations of sounds. As a term it can also carry a meaning devoid of any sound referent – for instance, one may regard 'the music' as the written notation for a given composition. Orchestral musicians commonly refer to 'the music' in this way, implying not the sound event but the musical score. Such terminology lends insight to the modes of thinking of those involved in musical performance and it is these with which I am concerned – extending an interest in music to that of musical thinking.

This can be related to a consideration of music as knowledge. Does 'the music', meaning the written score, give a musical composition some independent existence distinct from an actual performance? We could move on to view music as body of knowledge and to consider its relationship to other bodies of knowledge. We could then seek to identify its rules and structures, the way it is codified and delineated and, for instance, go on to examine the rules of classical harmony and counterpoint.

However, our notion and method of investigation of music would have to change radically if we were to divert our attention from musical structure, that is, the structuring of sound, to the social processes and structures associated with music-making. Why, for instance, in Western society has music-making become so specialised, largely the domain of 'musicians', and why for the bulk of the population has music become a commodity which is consumed largely outwith the context of live performance?

Another concern is the relationship between art and non-art and the application of the term to music, hence 'art music'. Is the term 'art' merely a synonym for 'elite'? Much of musicology has been primarily concerned with art music, meaning classical music, and it has taken the development of ethnomusicology to strip bare the ethnocentrism implicit in this terminology, placing the study of music in the context of the social systems within which the music is articulated. Much early ethnomusicology was confined to the study of non-Western musics and societies, and it is only recently that the return 'home' poses new problems. In modern Western societies musical systems must be understood in terms of a pluralistic society. The rise of a whole range of musical sub-cultures has fragmented the musical life of Western society, but the wider ambit within which these genres operate cannot be so segregated. While the existence of elite and non-elite may not be considered problematic, their interrelationship may well be. Rock music and opera are not located in the context of different societies; the practitioners of each are not separated in the same way that separates a modern rock fan from a (pre-Westernised) Kalahari bushman.

However, it is still common for music syllabuses to apply the adjective 'Western' to their musical subject matter while ignoring, or incorporating only tacit reference to, the vast body of folk and popular music also produced in the West. An evolutionary model of the historical development of music remains implicit but pervasive. Over eighty years ago Goddard (1908) described his work, *The Rise of Music*, as:

> a careful enquiry into the development of the art [of music] from its primitive puttings forth in Egypt and Assyria to its triumphant consummation in modern effect . . . of a new and perfect order of beauty resting upon our tempered system.

While more recent works on the history of Western tonal harmonic music are rarely so explicit, particularly with regard to such notions as perfection, it was Blacking (1973) who sought to refute the idea of an evolutionary model of musical change. His research shows how the music of the Venda in South Africa employs both pentatonic (five-note) and heptatonic (seven-note) scales. From the perspectives of Western classical theory it might be supposed that Venda music was in a mode of transition from a more simply structured pentatonic scale to a heptatonic one. However, Blacking's (1973: 57) careful investigation of the social and cultural evidence contradicts this:

> The Venda used a heptatonic xylophone and pentatonic reed pipes long before they adopted the pentatonic reed pipes of their neighbours the Pedi . . . According to evolutionary theories of music history, the Venda should be going backward – like the Chinese, who selected a pentatonic scale for their music although they knew and had used 'bigger and better' scales.

Various styles and traditions of music may develop certain sound elements over time but it is highly problematic to infer that one musical style or form is more complicated than another, let alone more advanced thus implying a series of developmental steps linking the world's musical systems. Different musical traditions accentuate the importance of certain sonic forms while at the same time depressing the significance of others. This is certainly the case for Western classical music, whose chief organising feature, until the advent of serial music, was the development of tonal structures and their relationship in harmonic counterpoint. This is not to suggest that other musics do not evidence the complicated entwining of melodic lines, but rather that the dominant feature of classical music is the development of harmonic relationships, and this at the expense of the elaboration of other sonic elements such as rhythm or timbre:

Orchestral 'effect' and tone colour, however varied and rich, were never an end in themselves, for the classical style subordinated all details to the one central idea of organic growth in which mere effects had no place unless they were in definite and logical relationship to the whole.

(Lang 1941: 711)

A sound is never enjoyed simply for its own sake. While, for instance, tone quality is important, its role is subsidiary, serving to 'solidify and set off the architectonic construction' (Lang 1941: 711). Because the expression of harmonic relationships became the paradigm for musical expression within this genre other elements of musical sound were relegated to subordinate roles, indeed to the point of attempts at the elimination of sounds without a notatable pitch referent.

Where the sociologist and anthropologist may enter into what has been hitherto a discussion of largely musicological interest is the question of what it is about given social systems that creates given musical systems. What wider social meanings are embodied in specific forms of musical organisation? Blacking (1973: 53) argues that:

if the value of music and culture is to be assessed, it must be described in terms of the attitudes and cognitive processes involved in its creation, and the functions and effects of the musical product in society. It follows from this that there should be close structural relationships among the function, content, and form of the music.

One of the most exciting recent developments in the sociology of music has been an examination of how social values have come to be represented not just in the social organisation of musical performance but also, and in consequence, in musical sound itself. Small (1977) shows how the main form of articulation of harmonic relationships, the movement of chords in progression, is related to the revolution in thinking triggered by the Renaissance. His argument is as follows. The pre-Renaissance painter painted from a God's eye view. Features were juxtaposed in a way that would be impossible for the individual eye to see so that the work of the painter presented not so much the perspective of an individual artist as that of a community. Perspective, the placing of elements in logical relationship from the point of view of an individual, did not develop until the advent of individual humanism and desacrilisation of nature which offered the necessary intellectual facility. For Small, tonal harmony can be regarded as the musical analogue of perspective because it springs from the same intellectual development. In both cases elements are subordinated to a logical framework where that logic comes to dominate the artistic process. The whole work becomes logically explicable and in a sense knowable.

A crucial development in the formation of harmony was the development of the triad, the combination of three pitches to form a chord. It is not that the simultaneous relationship of three pitches had not occurred before, but it is the notion of related triads in chord progressions that revolutionised musical thinking at this time. For the first time modulation, the transposition of melodies into different keys, became possible. Shepherd *et al.* (1977) examine this transformation and through it look specifically for elements of social structure in musical structures, that is, in sound itself. They are claiming not that music is socially *determined*, that a given type of social organisation will necessarily give rise to any specific musical system, but that wider meanings and structures will be found in the organisation of musical production and by implication will be discernible in the sounds produced. As the notion of universal laws and theories in the development of science led to the standard-isation of learning within various disciplines, so too in classical music there is a standardisation of technique.

Shepherd *et al.*'s argument is that a rigid uniformity of technique is employed to attain as near 'perfect' a rendition of a musical composition as possible. Just as scientific laws are thought of as having a fixed, invariable and independent existence, so a parallel is drawn with musical composition. The musical composition comes to be considered as an independent entity, independent of its realisation in specific and unique musical events. The musical score becomes 'the music' and in so doing becomes fixed and immutable.

This feature is not present in most other musical traditions where the revision of a 'piece' by performers, often in performance, is commonplace and wholesale revision over time is usual. Indeed, it is through this very process that stylistic variation occurs, and yet within classical music it would be unthinkable for, say regional styles of classical musical performance to evolve. For instance, in British classical musical education as much as possible is done to remove regional characteristics of singers' diction.

In Western society, as in any other, the organisation of musical sound is one of the ways through which shared meanings are articulated. Musical meaning is itself a component of all meaning. Music exists as one domain through which society is constructed, and musical meaning forms one medium through which joint values are celebrated. This is what Blacking (1987) means in defining the following terms:

> 'Musical thought' is a culturally defined process involved in composing, per-forming, listening and talking about what members of different societies categorize as special ('musical') symbol systems and social action. 'Musical intelligence' is the cognitive and affective equipment with which people make musical sense of the world.

In making musical sense of the world the social world is symbolically constructed through a medium of communication which is specifically non-verbal and musical. The organisation of musical sound itself forms part of the symbolic realm. The writings of Small and Shepherd *et al.* indicate how, in the West, classical music mediates and creates some of the symbolic order of Western society, and especially of one section of Western society. Moreover, the fact that this music is but a part of the musical life of the West is also essential to an understanding of the interaction of music and society. In the West other musical forms also exist, carry other meanings and articulate other symbolic orders, and furthermore, in the context of a pluralistic society, they do not do this in isolation from each other. In this book I argue for an understanding of musical communication as symbolic interaction. However, it is in the nature of the symbolic to be imprecise. I agree with Cohen's (1986: 3) considerations on the nature of the symbolic realm:

> Aspects of behaviour are, of course, elusive in their meanings. To call them 'symbolic' is to use a convenient device to mask imprecision. But we can take a step further still and say that it is in the nature of the symbolic to be imprecise: that if we could pin down the meanings of symbols, then the symbols would have become redundant, because we would have moved from the symbolic to the technical . . . The great danger for the unwary anthropologist is to use the label of 'symbolism' as a means of escape whenever confronted by a problem of meaning.

Though imprecise, the relationship between the form of the symbol and its symbolism, between structure and meaning, is fluid and yet not arbitrary. Cohen argues that it is possible for there to be contrary meanings to the same symbols. A given symbolic realm can take on new connotations, be articulated in different contexts, thereby creating different orders of meaning. But I would argue that it will, in the process, alter in form and structure. This is very apparent in musical symbolism. The celebration of hierarchy and the musical division of labour which are inherent in the structure of the symphony orchestra are indivisible from the symbolic meaning and hence the sounds produced. A different set of musical values – for instance, expressing the creative input of the musician and the lack of separation of composer and performer, or musical accessibility in contrast to the fetishising of technical virtuosity – could not readily import the structure of the classical orchestra. If these elements were to evolve within classical music then the form of the symphony orchestra would have to change, and, in consequence, so would the sounds produced. The symbol is not infinitely adaptable.

It is the case that pieces of music composed in the classical idiom have been performed by musicians from other genres. But the symbolism of this music then becomes very different from that induced in the context of its performance in a classical music event. However, it is not simply the context in which the music is presented that alters nor simply the symbolism, but also the form and therefore the sound.

I have said that the musical life of the West must be understood in terms of pluralism to take account of its diversity within given societies. This can be related to another important element in the structuring of symbols, that of boundary. Differing musical genres coexist in close cultural proximity. But in addition to representing symbolic order within themselves they also speak outwith themselves. This is a point brought out in Laing's (1985) study of punk rock. In punk the structuring of the performance creates a certain symbolic realm. The anti-elitism, the performance ethos that 'anyone can do it', the resistance to commercialism and 'selling out', the volume of the musical performances all structure meaning within. But a fundamental fact about the mid-1970s punk phenomenon was what it said without. It arose as a reaction to the inaccessibility of the commercial heights that popular music had reached. Early punk rock preached accessibility – 'Xerox music's here at last' was one of the Desperate Bicycles' slogans. Scritti Politti's first single even itemised the costs of producing 2,500 copies of that very record (Laing 1985: 17).

In attempting to grasp the nature of meaning in music it is not possible to separate a semantic element which is specifically musical from the wider transmission and articulation of meaning at musical events. We must disabuse ourselves of any notion of inherent meaning in music, even when, or perhaps especially when, the unravelling of musical meaning takes the form of decoding the message of a composer. Musical meaning is not communicated in a uni-directional manner but is constructed in performance. Musical meaning derives from the interpretation of musical performance during concrete musical events. It not does not exist in an abstract. Musical meaning is constructed from the recognition and structuring of sonic elements in the social context of their production and reception.

Much conceptual confusion surrounding the notion of musical meaning derives from specifically Western aesthetic considerations, particularly the separation of composer, performer and listener and the mistaken assumption that these can be equated with communicator, mediator and recipient of meaning. Where such explicit and uni-directional transmission of meaning does occur it is in very specific circumstances deriving from a shared musical syntax and highly specific socio-musical expectations. In such circumstances we may draw a close parallel to how certain syntactic structures order meaning in language, and then indeed, in music as in language, certain sound patterns may come to pertain to specific referents of the external world. This is also true when certain patterns of musical sound become associated with and induce a certain affective response, for instance, the general sadness of the minor mode in Western music. This is a result of a shared musical syntax. I will give another example.

I well remember a school music lesson concerning the dominant seventh chord. The music teacher told the class that the chord, because of its chief element, the dissonance of the minor seventh, creates a strong tension and homing influence leading to the need for the dissolution of the tension produced by means of resolution on the tonic. I remember him saying how odd it was that no musicologist, psychologist or acoustic scientist had been able to identify precisely what it was in this relationship of pitches that created this homing tendency. It was only much later that I realised why this was not so.

There is nothing in the relationship of pitches in the seventh chord on its own that creates a 'homing' tendency. It is only in the context of a specifically learned musical syntax that the structural elements of this chord have this effect in the context of the piece of music in which it is located. In other musical systems the relationship of pitches comprising the seventh chord is not considered dissonant, a term which in any case cannot be readily translated outwith the context of the Western tonal harmonic tradition. However, even where it is considered dissonant in the sense of producing tension, this does not necessarily imply the need for resolution, let alone resolution on a 'tonic'.

Any conception of resolution would be quite alien to a musical culture which did not have the notion of resolution upon key centres.

I offer a further example of the way in which specific sounds only acquire a given meaning within a given context. If we look at Figure 1, which represents the scale of G major we will see (yes, *see*) that the bracketed notes correspond exactly to the bracketed group of notes in the key of C major in Figure 2 (from Wright 1975: 24):

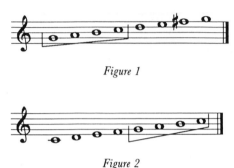

Figure 1

Figure 2

On their own the two groups of bracketed notes would be played and sound identical. However, if the whole series of notes in each figure is played the two bracketed notes would still be identical in terms of sounds produced but they would sound, that is to say, be perceived, differently. The only difference is in their relationship to the whole group of notes. The notes will 'mean' something different. So it can be with more complex musical structures. A whole Western musical work might be quite meaningful, say, to an Indian listener but in completely different terms to a Western listener. The meaning is not an inherent property of the musical object itself, that is, its sounds.

The articulation of musical meaning on the part of listeners cannot only be a 'receptive process' deriving from the social decoding of a work (Adorno 1973). Meaning is not only transmitted but also constructed in a musical (or any other social) event. Thus, to say that it is not possible to 'appreciate' a musical work without being able to 'understand' it is false, even more so when what is so often meant by this statement is the ability analytically to dissect and identify constituent sonic elements in an academic fashion. Lay listeners may have developed an ability to recognise or relate to such elements without being able consciously to articulate them in language. An interpretation may be structured in completely different terms by different listeners and made meaningful in those terms. Indeed, it is by such a process that sonic structures come to cross musico-cultural boundaries and, in new settings, articulate different orders of meaning.

Further misconceptions as to the nature of musical meaning have arisen from an over-concentration upon the notion of a musical event. The very concept of an event as being specifically musical is itself a product of a given form of Western musical thinking. Music can have a functionality extending far beyond notions of entertainment or appreciation:

> The concept of music as 'beautiful' seems to be generally undeveloped in primitive cultures. Informants speak of songs being 'good'. No doubt the prevailing functionality of music is responsible for this designation, for beauty is an end in itself, while 'good' implies usefulness for a specific purpose: a song may be good for curing, good for dancing, etc.
>
> (Nettl 1956)

Songs may be functional, performed as a means to certain ends and only become meaningful in those terms. The function of songs as a means of communicating social sanction has been recognised by Munro (1977) with respect to the 'bothy ballads' of North-East Scotland in which songs would circulate among itinerant farm workers giving warning of the deficiencies of certain farmers as employers. Among the Mapuche of Chile songs are used to 'blow off steam' – to call attention to some matter of personal concern to the singer (Merriam 1964). The Gaelic 'Land League' songs which arose during the rise of the Land League in the Highlands of Scotland in the late nineteenth century had a specifically politicising function in agitating the rural population. In a culture in which singing was still markedly active these songs emulated and accompanied the polemic of political speeches (Meek 1976).

However, although entertainment and leisure may be more highly segregated realms of activity in modern Western society than in many other cultures, the musical life of Western society may not be so separated from the functional elements outlined above as it might, on the surface, appear. This may be due to a conceptual separation of these activities which does not necessarily accord with their functional separation:

> We often accord to art music an edifying, educational role, believing that things of value can be learned from hearing Bach and Mozart. But it is also said that the function of music among the people of Yirkilla is essentially educational, and that they, like the Plains Indians, learned their culture gradually, symbolizing each step with appropriate music. Many other cultures conform to this pattern. Indeed, if we teach our children to go to concerts in order to learn the important values in their own culture, we are doing what the technologically much simpler people of Yirkilla and the Plains did with their music: use it to teach the important things about their own culture.
>
> (Nettl 1983: 148)

Nettl is in any case concerned at an over-separation of use and function in music:

> The line between uses and functions is clear when we observe that a particular Plains Indian song is used to accompany a Grass Dance but has the function of contributing to the integration of society. But it is not always so, for in the case of entertainment, use and function may be identical.
>
> (Nettl 1983: 148)

Conceptual confusion concerning the nature of musical meaning did much to retard the development of a sociology of music until the last fifteen years or so because of a widespread linking of sociologists' investigations of music to the specifically musicological value systems of the Western classical tradition. Thus Adorno, in his sociological consideration of musical systems, does not hide the greater musical worth he places upon classical music in comparison to the popular music of his time (the 1940s), which he describes as a form of 'commercialised depravity' (Adorno 1973).

He argues that jazz music exhibits a 'false consciousness', 'cramming' it into the people 'in the service of the naked profit motive'. While it is important to incorporate the role of the music industry into an understanding of the meaning of popular music, as for instance do Lee (1970) and Harker (1980), can we in fact operate sociologically Adorno's notions of 'commercialised depravity' and 'false consciousness' of music? Should we confine these ascriptions of musical value to musicological explanations, or should we go further still? Can a sociological understanding of musical meaning and communication restructure our musicological understanding of it so that value-laden descriptions are no longer operable either musicologically or sociologically? I believe this is the case. In arguing for a sociology of musical styles, Shepherd (1987) claims that it is no longer possible to operate notions of musical value since different musical structures articulate different forms of meaning. The existence of different musical syntaxes which are themselves both derivative and constitutive of the different ways that music and society interrelate implies that the sound structures of one musical system do not make the same sense if understood from within the structure of another. Western classical music is not better or worse than other musical systems but communicates (and constitutes) different social meanings.

However, Shepherd *et al.* argue that while this viewpoint may not now be so contentious within the sociology of music, this is not the case for academic musicology because of its profound implications for musical education. The dominance of Western classical music in educational curricula depends precisely upon its perceived superiority as a musical system to, say, 'popular' or 'folk' music. Shepherd *et al.*, following Williams (1958), argue that the ideology of much Western musical education is embraced within a notion of art as an approach to essential reality, aspiring to notions of truth and beauty. But it is this threat to the centrality of classical music in music education which is hindering the development of a genuine collaboration between musicologists and social scientists and the cross-fertilisation of musicological and sociological perspectives.

I came across a good example of such resistance in one of the few existing cross-disciplinary (music/sociology) approaches to understanding musical life (Mark 1981). In this volume, Etzkorn recognises the threat that the very popularity of 'popular' music poses to the central position of classical music in music education and uses this article within the context of such a volume to justify the orthodox position:

While serious music attracts a considerable volume of activity in the United States, the public involvement in popular or vernacular music is even more extensive. It is difficult to draw hard and fast lines which would demarcate serious musicians from vernacular musicians since the skills and expertise of serious musicians include those required by the vernacular genre . . . Contemporary American music nevertheless requires more of its serious musicians, be they creators, performers or audiences, in the line of musical sophistication and competency than is required for vernacular musicians. . . .

(Etzkorn 1981)

However, it is a lacking on the part of 'serious' musicians to identify musical elements in 'vernacular' music that are not celebrated within classical music that allows such statements to be made. That any 'vernacular' music can be subsumed within classical music and played competently by classical musicians is a notion preposterous to most musicians in these genres. Because classical musicians such as Etzkorn believe these musics to be a simpler version of their own they are led only to seek understanding in the musi-cological terms of their own musical tradition. It thus follows that when they do attempt to play these musics without, ironically, any 'serious' attempt to acquire the detailed knowledge and understanding necessary to ensure competence within these traditions, their attempts are generally perceived as miserable failures, other, that is, than by fellow classical musicians. Such music appears 'easy' only because of their failure to recognise and hence reproduce many of the structural elements by which the music is made meaningful.

Classical music is more complex than what Etzkorn terms 'vernacular' musics, but only in the structural terms of classical music – for instance, in terms of tonal harmony. In terms of polyrhythm, or vocal inflexion, or impro-visation, or musical creativity by performers (as opposed to composers) – to give but four examples of features which are extensively developed by some of these traditions and comprise the structural elements through which they are understood – most classical music is exceedingly simple.

This may seem a deviation from social science, but such musicological considerations are necessary in understanding the power of musical ideologies. It may seem that I am being harsh on classical music, but the proponents of classical music are not very different from their 'vernacular' fellows in one way – the central value, special significance and superiority, and the rational-isation for such views, which adherents of all these musics tend to afford to their own musical dispositions.

A far more interesting sociological question concerning the treatment of the inherent value or worth of music is to ask, not what is it that defines music as 'serious', 'fine', 'art', or whatever, but to ask who does the defining and why? For Truzzi (1978: 285) an important starting point for sociologists in an examination of art should be (but generally is not) 'a description of which groups label what products how'.

This is certainly not a criticism which could be levelled at Shepherd and Vulliamy (1983), who examine the use of classical music in the school class-room and search for reasons for its dominance in music education. They argue that it is the failure on the part of musical educators to understand the terms through which pupils understand and make sense of non-classical music which accounts for the 'culture clash' within the school music classroom. They challenge the assumption that 'serious' music incorporates within itself 'objective' or 'absolute' criteria by which all music can be judged and ranked in terms of worth:

> the 'objective' or 'absolute' criteria in terms of which all music tends to be judged, are directly derived from a system of analytic notation which has shaped the musical perception of 'high culture' musicians and critics alike. Whereas functional tonality displays a set of fixed and precisely notatable pitches and rhythmic patterns, idealised timbres and a harmonic framework which forms the basis for an explicit and essentially abstract 'philosophical' argument, Afro-American influenced 'popular' musics display a harmonic and rhythmic framework which provides the context for more immediate personal statements articulated through melodic, harmonic, and rhythmic inflections, improvised melodic materials and 'dirty' individualistic timbres.
>
> (Shepherd and Vulliamy 1983: 5)

They argue that notation serves as an ideological tool in the mystification of the experiential world:

> It is this reduction of all musical possibilities to a finite number of tightly controlled analytically notatable elements that has facilitated the extensional or outward building of impersonally philosophical, complex pieces of music. The immediate, the personal and the social in music is effectively filtered out.
>
> (Shepherd and Vulliamy 1983: 14)

In Shepherd and Vulliamy's work I believe that we see a genuine sociology of music emerging. Forms of musical organisation themselves encode wider ideologies; music is itself constitutive of our social world. We can no longer accept pejorative ascriptions of musical value within accounts offering sociological interpretations of music. It is for this reason that I prefer attempts by White (1987) and Taylor (1978) to that of Adorno (1973) in offering a social scientific understanding of jazz. Taylor also recognises that an understanding of the role of the music industry is important in understanding the articulation of jazz in its social setting, that is, its use, function and meaning to the actors involved.

Taylor argues that our understanding of jazz is inextricably entwined within the evolution of the music in its social setting, including the cash nexus. Jazz evolved as a music of American blacks and articulated a complicated, but intrinsically mocking, response to white domination (and white music). Jazz has 'meant' different things to different people at different times, even to the same people at the same time, for instance from the relatively 'straight' jazz of the dance hall to its role in exclusive 'hot jazz' sessions after the dance had finished. Taylor stresses that as the social settings and significance of the music change so does the music itself. As jazz has been slowly incorporated into white culture it has changed; the jazz of an 1870s Louisiana brothel is not the same as the jazz of a 1970s 'recital' in either form, content or meaning.

However, Taylor does not argue that jazz becomes somehow less jazz because it is articulated through the cash nexus. But it has taken the detailed researches of Harker to show that, even for musical forms which were thought to be largely uncontaminated by the cash nexus, this was often not the case. In a recent article (1987) he indicates that much of the English folk 'tradition', for long considered to contain elements of an unbroken oral tradition, has been extensively mediated, as far back as the sixteenth century, by commercial interests in song transmission. There is probably no surviving musical system (in the West at least) that could not be dismissed as 'commercialised depravity' in Adorno's terms. Although all Western musics interlocute with the cash nexus, they do so in highly differing and specialised ways, ways which are themselves tightly bound to the expression of the musical meanings they articulate. This is one of my central arguments and in this book I seek to show how the articulation of this relationship within the British folk scene is central to the nature of musical performance within it.

Musical meaning is itself partially constituted by a whole series of extra-musical and non-musical phenomena. People come to appreciate music, that is, the music becomes meaningful to them, through a whole series of preconceived notions that they bring to bear upon the musical setting. If these are not held in common then the same music will be 'heard' differently. These features may be musical (that is, they exist in sound) or non-musical (everything else). As Blacking (1973: 62) asks: 'Could "Soul" music affect Black Americans if its forms were not associated with a whole set of extra-musical experiences which Black Americans share?'

But music also articulates meaning and is itself partially constitutive of our social world and forms a means by which meaning is created. The articulation of this meaning does not only reside in the production of certain sound structures but is produced in musical performance, itself a product of a constellation of behavioural acts, musical and non-musical. Meaning does not flow from a performer to an audience but is created within performance. To grasp the nature of musical meaning we have to go beyond the notion of intentionality in musical expression. So where does this meaning reside, and can we isolate a specifically musical cognitive component?

To say that music constitutes its own meaning is to duck the question. Music does not merely engender a personal affective response but is quintessentially social. But a problem in trying to specify musical meaning is that it is a form of meaning which is implicit, that is, can be sensed in consciousness, but which cannot be referred to specifically in language. This is Seeger's (1976) point, what he terms the 'musicological juncture' being a confusion rendered in language and deriving from the difficulties of attempting to pin down the essence of one mode of communication through the medium of another. I would be the first to agree that in attempting to understand musical performance within the British folk scene I stand at Seeger's 'juncture'. I am trying to translate one medium of communication (musical performance) into another (text), and recognise the extreme difficulty in doing so.

This discussion is close to Levi-Strauss's (1971) notion of 'secondary rationalisation' in discussing myth. Indeed, Levi-Strauss closely equates myth and music, since both myth (coded schemes of images) and music (coded schemes of sounds) are not directly transferrable into other modes of communication (see also Hopkins 1977). However, if we divest ourselves of the notion that reality is delineated primarily in language and instead view language, music and all modes of human interaction as themselves constructing the symbols through we which we make the world meaningful, we can accept reality as socially constructed. Music is one constituent element of the 'social construction of reality' (Berger and Luckmann 1971).

Unlike language, the referents of musical meaning do not directly relate, or only very rarely, to concrete items in the external world. Music has no nouns – but it does have a syntax, a grammar and articulates meaning. But in language, too, the direct representation of concrete items of external reality forms only one element of discourse. Both music and language share many communicative features – for instance, those of phatic communion (Malinowski 1923), 'grooming talk' (Van Hoof 1962; Morris 1967) and symbolic manipulation – and almost certainly share the same origins in the species development of the pre-linguistic utterances of our hominid ancestors (Nettl 1983).

Though I have given much attention in the foregoing to an understanding of the social in music, my concern is not only to understand music but also to understand genre, and one genre in particular, the British folk scene. A key element will be to look at the role of music in structuring the coherence of the genre. It is through a specific musical affinity that the genre finds its identity and derives its coherence. But music is only one means by which groups of people focus their identity, and many of the considerations which I have afforded so far to music could apply similarly in the other arts, and indeed outwith them. Many studies of sport (see, for example, Critcher 1971), or of other cultural manifestations, such as motorbike culture (Willis 1978), have striking parallels with sociological attempts to understand music.

Music has homologies in non-music just as non-musical cultural artefacts have homologies in music. The relationship between a musical form as a symbol and the meaning it articulates on the part of its adherents is arbitrary in one sense, that the symbolic order it manifests could be articulated in some other cultural artefact; but in another sense it is far from arbitrary – once the members of the genre articulate shared meanings through a given symbol, say as music, the musical form does not merely acquire connotations of the symbolic order, but structurally articulates it. The relationship of form to meaning is not arbitrary, the symbols are not interreplaceable. The relationship of punk to punks, of opera to a segment of the upper middle class, is mutually interdependent.

Musical taste is neither arbitrary nor personal but social. However, musical taste is not the mere homology of socio-economic class locations. There is no music of the middle class, the working class or any class fraction. This is because symbols are themselves malleable and can even appeal to more than one social group. But musical taste is class-dependent in that it associates with socio-economic class. This apparent contradiction has fuelled much of the debate concerning 'sub-culture'. In modern Western society, musical systems are no longer encapsulated within social formations. Adherents of musical genres – say, 'folkies' who attend folk clubs and folk festivals – do not merely live in a wider society in the sense that they do not sing, play and listen to folk music all the time, but they inhabit a social world, partake of social events, perhaps even including events within other musical genres, and relate to people who are not 'folkies' and in so doing for much of the time actually cease to be 'folkies'.

More than for any other social formation at any other time in history, culture is no longer something we possess but something we choose (Cohen 1985). But this does not mean to say that the determination of this choice is asocial. In this context who does the choosing becomes an interesting focus for attention. The existence of genres as structurally bounded cultural entities residing within one social formation, but which vary in so wholesale a manner as to provide the appearance of a whole gamut of differing cultures within a culture, sets up its own problematic. The challenge for the social scientist is to find out what provides the coherence of various genres, to probe what they mean, not just within themselves but also to examine how they fit into the wider cultural system of which they are a part.

2   *A Personal Note*

I had been involved in the folk scene long before I undertook this study, and it is important to record the influence that involvement had on this book. My first visit to a folk club occurred as a young teenager when my father suggested I go with him to the local club where he was a regular attender. I agreed, with some misgivings if I remember, because socialising with one's parents was certainly not the done thing.

I think it was the first time that I had gone, of my own volition, to a social event that did not involve my school friends or the kids in the neighbourhood. Certainly it was the first time my father had invited me to a social event as if I was an adult, and not in the patronising way that I was used to, when I would be allowed to stay up at New Year and be offered a small sherry, or taken along with my sister to a party, allowed to mingle with the company only to be shunted off to a bedroom to play with the usually much younger children of the house. So, with somewhat ambivalent feelings, I went with him.

My home town is Southend-on-Sea, a medium-sized English town that has undergone a massive physical and social transformation during the last hundred years. It is splayed out along the north bank of the River Thames, and has grown to subsume the satellite towns of Hadleigh, Rochford, Rayleigh and Benfleet. It is not a town with a historic core. Instead, being so close to London, it grew up as one of the first fashionable seaside resorts. From the early years of this century its social trajectory has been downward. Its easy accessibility soon destroyed any veneer of exclusivity and it became a resort for day-trippers from the East End of London. With the slum clearance of the East End after the war, Southend became a favourite choice for relocation and large numbers of people, my family included, moved down.

Southend still has its Victorian esplanade but the town behind has utterly changed. The centre was redeveloped in the 1960s in the fashion of architectural 'brutalism' that so effectively changed the face of urban Britain in the space of a single generation. The perimeter of the town is dotted with upmarket developer-built housing schemes, but within some of the villages now absorbed into the continuous built-up area, the old core has survived. It was in one of these, Benfleet, that the folk club met.

We drove down the steep hill dividing the new town at the top from the old town at the bottom which is situated right by the water's edge beside the muddy but navigable creek which separates Benfleet from Canvey Island. Just two miles away on Canvey, gleaming in the night air, were the flare stacks of Europe's largest petro-chemical complex.

But on this side of water was the little huddle of weather-boarded houses, two pubs and a church that still form the heart of Benfleet, remaining relatively unscathed by the onslaught of twentieth-century development. Even the local cockling industry has survived. Cockle boats still work out of Benfleet and Leigh-on-Sea, providing a pungent reminder that the area has not been completely satellised as a dormitory town for London.

The folk club met in the older of the two pubs, the Hoy and Helmet. A 'hoy' is the local term for a small cockle boat. The pub was a timber-framed, seventeenth-century construction and its decoration was unpretentious. It had been furnished in an early twentieth-century fashion: basic English pub furniture, red patterned Edwardian style embossed wallpaper and a few horse-brasses and other period ornaments. My impression was of an unassuming building gently being moved into line with the times, neither an archaic relic nor tarted up. It was quiet, but as to more detail my memory becomes hazy, probably due to the fact that being only thirteen years old I was too young to be legally on licensed premises and was whisked straight through the bar to the backroom where the folk club met.

This was a small square room holding about fifty people at the back of the pub right up against the street. Passers-by could be heard walking past the window, and lorries and buses caused the room to wobble and shake. The shape of the room and its smallness relative to the number present meant that when we were all seated the room was full, except that in the middle of the room at the front, or rather at the opposite end from the entrance, because the room could not be deemed to have any especially aligning features, there was a patch of bare floorspace. But it was what occurred in that small room that was a revelation to me. People sang. They sang to each other, without a stage, without amplification, with no special clothes, and with no special flourish which said 'we are performers'. The evening comprised individuals standing up and giving songs, and occasionally a tune or a tale or two, with every member of the audience joining in the choruses. Those present entertained themselves.

I had never seen music presented in this way. I had never come across people singing to each other. Certainly I had come across singing and playing. I had been to concerts. I had been a very brief member of a school choir and I had been to parties and to a youth club where we sat about, danced, drank and cuddled to records. But this was something altogether different and I was amazed. I had never been to a social event whose *raison d'être* was to make music. At that time in my life social events used music, provided by records, or occasionally by a radio, as a background to socialising which was mediated through talk.

To me at that time live music was both formal and inaccessible. At concerts I had heard performers on stage whom I had never met nor expected to meet, and whose artistry and presentation rendered the act of music-making something 'other', like flying a jumbo jet. The only other context where I had come across music-making as something which could be done by myself or my peers, was at school and scout camp where we were cajoled into singing songs or let loose on percussion instruments. For me live music-making seemed either amateurish and distasteful, or else inaccessible. And that was the extent of my musical socialisation.

This folk club was something quite outwith my experience. There seemed to be many odd features. Many of the songs were old, referring to events and happenings of long ago, and some were sung in local dialect. There was also a singer or two singing contemporary songs by Bob Dylan and so on, but it was this older, or older-seeming body of songs which dominated. Their subjects were mostly of rural England or the sea. But those singing these songs were not 'old boys' and they certainly were not the cockle fishers coming in for a pint and a song after a day out on the estuary. They were people very like my dad, lecturers, teachers or people who had jobs in London, who spoke with a London or BBC accent, not the local Essex idiom, and who were fairly young, mainly in their twenties and thirties.

But at this time it was not these latter realisations which impressed me but the encounter with direct face-to-face music-making. It had a profound effect on my life. I became attracted to music as something I could do and something which could be entered into socially and for fun. I learned to play the fiddle, continued to attend folk clubs, though not regularly until an adult. The social in music continued to fascinate me; the fact that different musics and different musical events are not just different sound events but different social events. This study is thus in essence an attempt on my part to systemise some of the impressions and thoughts first generated that evening over twenty years ago in the back room of a small Essex pub.

In the next chapter I examine the development of the British folk revival of the late 1950s and 1960s, focusing principally upon its ideological basis and social coherence.

3   History and Ideology

The aim of this chapter is to place the British folk scene in historical context. Others have chronicled the folk revival (Lloyd 1967; Laing *et al*. 1975; Woods 1979; Munro 1984). My intention is not to duplicate these efforts but to indicate some ideological and artistic forces which created and moulded the folk revival of the 1950s and 1960s through to the present day.

The revival of older musical forms is not a uniquely modern innovation. It has a well–documented tradition in Britain going back to Robert Burns and beyond. In England there was a considerable upsurge of interest in traditional and folk music around the turn of the century. This was not an exercise entered into on artistic and aesthetic criteria alone, as indicated by the following comments of Cecil Sharp (1907: 135–6), one of the leading folk song enthusiasts of this time:

> Our system of education is, at present, too cosmopolitan; it is calculated to produce citizens of the world rather than Englishmen. And it is Englishmen, English citizens that we want. How can this be remedied? By taking care I would suggest, that every child born of English parents is, in its earliest years, placed in possession of all those things which are distinctive products of its race ... The discovery of English folk-song, therefore, places in the hands of the patriot, as well as of the educationalist, an instrument of great value. The introduction of folk songs into our schools will not only affect the musical life of England; it will also tend to arouse that love of country and pride of race the absence of which we now deplore.

The desire to revive folk song is itself an ideological statement. The artistic developments of modernism and folk song revival were also adopted by the Nazis. In the United States the folk song revival acquired subversive connotations. Perris (1985: 202) reports that on 7 August 1963 the Fire and Police Research Association of Los Angeles sent a resolution to the United States House of Representatives requesting that the Committee on Un-American Activities:

investigate Communist subversive involvement in the Folk Music Field, that the continued effective misuse of this media . . . may not be further used as an un-identified tool of Communist Psychological or Cybernetic Warfare to ensnare and capture youthful minds in the United States as it has so successfully and effectively captivated them abroad.

This is quite different from the bourgeois search for a 'national music' as was the case for the folk song revival associated with Cecil Sharp. The grand claims for folk song in English culture, as Sharp envisaged, were not realised. It left a legacy in schools where highly edited and bowdlerised versions of folk songs found their way into classroom music books. Composers such as Vaughan Williams took English folk song and arranged it for orchestra, piano and voice. The English Folk Dance and Song Society, originally founded as The Folk Song Society in 1898, has also survived to the present day. However, this revival never really caught the imagination of either the bourgeoisie or the working class and it is in the 1950s that, by and large, the story of the British folk song revival can again be picked up in terms of a widespread cultural revival. It is this latter revival which is generally termed 'the folk revival'. However, it was not the earlier revival from the time of Cecil Sharp which formed the dynamic impetus of this later revival from the 1950s onwards. It is important to stress that this revival had its antecedents not in Britain but in the USA, from those revival singers who had so aroused the ire of the Los Angeles Fire and Police Association.

The American folk song revival derived from two sources. On the one hand, it was the beneficiary of government support. Thousands of field recordings of 'traditional' singers and musicians were undertaken and made available to far wider audiences than would ever have been possible from direct oral transmission. The effect was dramatic. The ready transmission of source material led to an upsurge of the singing of this material, and the learning of related instruments such as the banjo. But this folk material was also seized on by many of those active in the trade unions and was tailored to political purposes at the height of the depression. Access to the music of ordinary people singing of hard times was utilised in the development of an expressly left-populist song culture.

Performers including Pete Seeger and Woodie Guthrie at the forefront of this revival also composed their own material based upon folk singing traditions, material which was of an expressly political content. During the 1940s and 1950s concern with the roots of music continued to be prominent throughout the United States. All forms of traditional music were seized upon and adapted to specific purposes. This applied especially to jazz, the blues and what is now referred to as the 'Old Timey' music of the Appalachians which evolved in myriad directions spawning the various forms of country music, from country and western through to bluegrass, western swing and so on.

The influence of revivals of blues and jazz in the 1930s and 1940s in the United States through radio and record releases had influenced later revivals in Britain. These two represented important precursors of the folk revival. Both revivals had been concerned with exploring origins and roots, albeit American rather than British. However, there were those in Britain who started to look towards British origins in an attempt to rekindle interest in British folk song.

In 1942 a BBC radio programme, 'Country Magazine', broadcast traditional songs sung by the 'source' singers from whom they were collected, and aroused considerable interest. One effect was that many listeners wrote in to the programme saying they knew of these songs from local sources and the programme sparked off a new wave of song collecting. The belief of Sharp and many of the early song collectors that they were collecting the very last death-throes of the English song tradition was far from being the case. The discovery that there were extant song traditions in the British isles aroused the interest of such people as Ewan MacColl, Hamish Henderson and Bert Lloyd who each had a profound impact upon the evolution of the British folk revival. MacColl was one of the very first to set up a folk club, the Ballads and Blues Club, in 1953. However, it was not the discovery of the native tradition which initially provided the spark for the extraordinary ascent of the folk movement in the late 1950s. This again was prompted by a development in the United States, namely the skiffle craze which burst upon the British music scene with the unexpected chart success of Lonnie Donegan's skiffle version of 'Rock Island Line' in 1956. As a musical form skiffle became enormously popular in the two years between 1956 and 1958 and played a very important role in the development of the folk revival.

Fred Woods (1979: 53–4), who was himself involved in the skiffle movement, describes it as follows:

> The music was played in cellars and coffee bars throughout the land on a variety of instruments including tea-chest basses and washboards. The musical quality was not, by my memory, particularly high, but it was new, it was refreshing and – above all – it was enthusiastic, and it was a welcome gale of fresh air after the plastic performances of the crooners . . . It was cheap to get a band together, the music was gutsy, strongly rhythmic and intentionally rough, so that the odd wrong chord was hardly crucial. And it had about it an excitement that was new, as well as offering an opportunity to perform instead of being performed at.

The music became extremely popular. Thus, for instance, Woods notes that at the all-Scotland skiffle championship of 1957 and the East Anglian championship of 1958 there were over a hundred entries. It was this craze which led to a wave of musical instrument purchases across Britain, especially of guitars. The music celebrated 'do-it-yourself' values and made a virtue out of lack of musical polish. A contemporary account well sums up:

> A skiffle group, in its British meaning, is a band to accompany the single singing guitarist, or more rarely banjoist; they give him exaggerated rhythmic support on a variety of instruments – other guitars, a bass to thump and a washboard to strum, rattles, drums, whistles, anything you like so long as it looks as if it had been assembled on a rubbish dump.
>
> (Gersh 1959)

The movement celebrated music making for general participation. Lack of musical ability was not a criterion for exclusion. It formed itself into clubs which provided venues for the performance of this music on a week-to-week basis. Gersh (1959) gives a vivid description of a skiffle club providing an interesting pointer to the emergence of the folk revival proper out of the demise of the skiffle craze:

> Already, therefore, skiffle is developing as many separate streams and rivulets as British jazz. First there are those who seek to wed it to the folk singing tradition, especially to a revived British folksong. Next come the skiffle purists, who like to play nothing but genuine Leadbelly and early Donegan, with a comparatively relaxed beat. But in most public places, the newly opened Skiffle cellar in Greek Street, Soho, for instance, cheerful catholics open their arms to everything that comes. Here, down the usual dusty stairs in a disused night club with plaster stalactites hanging from the ceiling, a platform is provided for the hundreds of little suburban and provincial groups, making the journey to London to seek fame. These groups mix it all in – folksong, blues, fiddle, and jug music, 'pops', sentimental ballads and calypsos. Here, too, the usual chastened audience is joined in by a new element of ornate Teddies and their girls, who cannot sing or play but can dance wonderfully. So dance they do, on sagging boards and concrete at the back of the club, to skiffle and everything else that comes. The newer skiffle groups do not distinguish between skiffle and rock 'n' roll, submerging them all in the same breathless din . . .

By early 1959 the craze associated with the specific musical form of skiffle, the bands with the tea-chest basses, washboards and so on, had burned itself out. But the national enthusiasm for self-made music on the part of British youth had not. It was at this time that the political and protest songs that had followed in the wake of the American folk song revival started to make an impact.

Karl Dallas, one of those closely involved, singled out the first Aldermaston march of 1958 as a milestone in the formation of the early folk scene (Laing *et al.* 1975). This march was characterised by mass singing, both on the march itself and at the rallies which followed such as that in Trafalgar Square. It was at this time that the first wave of folk clubs were set up. These followed on from skiffle clubs and the coffee bars where skiffle was performed. In fact many of the first folk clubs met in coffee bars. But Woods (1979) points out that it was at this exact time that, for British audiences, the enthusiasm for American and protest songs started to wane. However, it is pertinent to note that the first generation of folk clubs in fact pre-dated large-scale interest in the British folk 'tradition'. The interest came rapidly afterwards though, a theme also picked up on by many of my informants. Some of them even seemed apologetic about their non-'traditional' performing origins. This is Ian MacCalman of The MacCalmans, a Scottish folk band:

> I did the thing with the skiffle. A lot of the people who got involved in folk music had a basis in jazz-cum-skiffle. It all connected then and my brothers and me sang together. I got a guitar, met Hamish and Derek in '64 at art college where an awful lot of music came from . . . Archie Fisher, Hamish Imlach, they all came from the same school where they had a guy who was interested in the music. And the Corries – the Edinburgh School of Art the same as us. It's not a particularly great answer because it's nothing to do with the tradition.

Whilst MacColl and Lloyd in England and Hamish Henderson in Scotland were proselytising on behalf of the native British folk traditions, this did not form the impetus for the very first clubs, with the exception of MacColl's own Ballads and Blues club which had been formed in 1953. The political link was crucial. The first generation of folk club organisers were not especially aware of British traditional music. Throughout Britain it had been the stirring of feeling associated with Aldermaston and the subsequent growth of CND which provided the impetus for many people to get together and sing. Myra Abbott, founder of the Hoy at Anchor folk club, Southend, in 1961, describes how the folk club came about after a concert held in aid of CND:

> It was a disaster – undisciplined. They thought they just had to get together and they would have a folk club. It was for singing between marches; that was its organising ethos. But a lot of non-CND talent came.

The Hoy at Anchor was typical of this first generation of folk clubs. It was set up by people who were politically active. Myra Abbott was a Communist and active trade unionist. She had also been involved in jazz, blues and skiffle clubs. But she then touches on a point which is crucial with regard to understanding this musical revival sociologically. It was not just the musical content or the musical style of its production that was crucial, but also control of the performance setting. Up until this time virtually all musical events which were presented as performances and for which payment was required had been organised by some form of promoter. But a part of the impetus for forming the first folk clubs was as much a different form of control over musical performance as it was a setting for a certain musical form, style or genre. She points out that although the club was created to provide:

> a platform for people to perform folk music and for people to listen, we had very little idea of what constituted folk music and its strands. We were very into causes but disillusioned after '56. The revival of the folk scene took this place. Its main ethos was uncommercial music – we wanted to provide an alternative.

Though in aim uncommercial, the early folk clubs quickly turned away from these undisciplined musical gatherings. Attention to organisation became a priority and from these anarchic early gatherings Myra Abbott claims she learned the value of organisation:

> We started . . . a committee which democratically ran the club. I looked after the musical standards [though] I was only one step ahead of them. We had a singers' workshop at my home every week. I would help people technically. We had Polly on the door who hiked out the druggies and this took off. . . We had to establish audience discipline through an MC and made it clear that singers had to be respected. Occasionally a singer stopped and there'd be violent, obscene language, even from the platform.

She points out that she was strongly opposed to this treatment of singers although this attitude did not last long. Club nights soon came to be characterised by 'pin drop silence'. In a very short period the folk clubs had become very different from the skiffle clubs. There was an extremely self-conscious attempt to change the social dynamics of performance. This is apparent from the treatment of singers who forgot their words. Informants reported that no longer was heckling of a malicious type acceptable. Instead we see concern for musical standards, the setting up of committees, song workshops and 'residents'. A resident was a person appointed by the committee who was recognised as one of the more experienced performers. Along with the title came a number of obligations, the main one being to turn up regularly and be available to sing if called upon to do so. There would thus be a pool of better singers for the MC to draw on to ensure the continuity of the night.

At this time the folk clubs had few guest performers, usually only three or four a year. At Southend and other clubs the role of resident singer was a mark of status. At the Bridge folk club in Newcastle the residents sat on the stage for the whole night facing the audience, remaining there even when a floor performer was singing. A floor performer is someone who has literally come up from the audience to perform.

As more attention was paid to the presentation of performance and musical standards in folk clubs, there was a drift in musical repertoire. Derek Theobold, another founder member of and resident at the Hoy at Anchor folk club, describes what the club was like at this time and the pressure for change:

> When the folk song club was first formed there were so many American imitators and it all seemed rather false; there were the bluegrass groups and the Joan Baez and Pete Seeger imitators ... Everyone put on American accents and then about '64 Pete Seeger came over and there was a weekend festival at Cecil Sharp House and he gave a talk and said it was very flattering to hear all these people imitating the American songs and he emphasised that you have a strong tradition of your own and it's well worth exploring, and Cyril Tawney was another one that pointed in that direction.

Cyril Tawney was one of the first performers who toured the folk clubs and was one of the first guests at the Hoy at Anchor. He had been at sea for many years and picked up a large number of traditional songs as well as writing many of his own, although these were written very much outwith the context of the folk revival. Myra Abbott describes the impact his visit had upon the club:

> From the money we were collecting at the door we soon had enough to do more. Every three months or so we paid an artist to come down and one was Cyril Tawney. We felt, whilst we'd set it up as a counter culture to commercial music we felt we were becoming commercial, for instance were we going to pay the residents? We were too money-conscious. We were wrestling about where we were going. We put up the guests – talked to the early hours, that's how we learned about the tradition. Cyril said: 'You have a good club here – are you not interested in your own culture ... the music of your own culture, the style people sing in?' ... So in a short while we found a new reason, one much more difficult to achieve ...

These early folk club guests made a huge impression. It was they who first looked to expand their repertoires from native British sources, and by travelling around Britain helped to gained wide currency for their ideas. It was at this time that the groundwork of establishing interest by *Country Magazine*, Ewan MacColl, Bert Lloyd, Peter Kennedy, and others, paid off and struck a chord which resounded throughout Britain. A key factor was a new radio programme, 'As I Roved Out', specifically dealing with traditional music transmitted by the BBC at Kennedy's instigation. Folk club singers seized upon the new body of material and more folk clubs sprang up all over Britain. It is reported that by 1961 there were at least 45 clubs (*Spin*, vol. 1, no. 2, 1962), and folk singer Rory McEwen (1965) records that four years later there were 300.

Countless new singers were drawn in around the turn of the 1950s and 1960s, many of whom went on to become the backbone of the professional and semi-professional folk club touring circuit, singers like Martin Carthy, Peter Bellamy, Dave Burland and Roy Bailey. Though these singers and others like them came to specialise in traditional folk music, it was not folk music that had first brought them in. It was developments in other musics, and especially skiffle, that provided the bedrock from which the traditional music revival could arise. Roy Bailey, a semi-professional singer, explains:

> I started off with piano lessons and I sang popular stuff at eleven. I got into trad jazz in the late 1950s and I sat in with bands. Skiffle – that's when I began public performances. In 1959 I went to university and met up with Dave Cousins of the Strawbs. He helped teach me the guitar – Leadbelly stuff, Spencer Davis. I formed the Leicester folk song club in 1961. I was a resident singer. I transposed my skiffle interest to British traditional music. I wanted to sing and commercial music seemed light years away. The only place to sing was this folk scene. Popular music was made popular and accessible by skiffle. You didn't have to be an incredible musician ... With skiffle it was 'we could do it' and the folk club was on the back of skiffle. They were American folk songs we sang then and we thought 'we've got some too'. MacColl and Lloyd's serious approach – we got to hear them.

Several strands intermingle here. On the one hand interest in native traditional music was spreading rapidly, and on the other hand clubs had grown out of a desire for 'ordinary' people to perform in settings which were not controlled by the music business or any form of entrepreneur. A rapid transition was taking place. The skiffle craze had ended and from the wild abandonment of the skiffle clubs the 'serious' approach of the early folk club movement took over.

Many informants picked up on the fact that this music was seized upon in a very different way from blues, jazz and skiffle. It was treated with a reverence and seriousness that marked itself off from these other musics and not surprisingly, given that blues, jazz and American songs still dominated the folk clubs, there were conflicts. There arose a feeling that something 'precious' had been uncovered in the native British folk traditions, something that needed to be protected and nurtured. British traditional music was stylistically quite different, and in order to counter what they saw as a prevailing mid-Atlanticism many clubs adopted measures to promote a very English, and in Scotland a Scottish, idiom.

Myra Abbott describes how in the early 1960s, as the person in charge of the club's music policy, she imposed a rigid discipline of style. In her singing workshops great attention was given to 'authentic' traditional style and in the club this had to be rigidly imposed until it became established. She operated a form of vetting procedure in which singers had to attend her singing workshops before they were allowed to perform at the club. This change in musical direction could not accommodate those who were mainly into blues and other American music, and consequently a division arose within the folk club, and the bulk of the audience left for an American-orientated club. An audience of only thirty remained, although this soon increased again after the schism.

I have referred to the Hoy at Anchor folk club on several occasions because events there were typical of events in other parts of Britain. Around 1961 those interested in American and other musics were either squeezed out or clear-cut divisions of clubs occurred. Folk clubs moved over to the native British tradition in a big way and those clubs which formed at this time were created with the specific intention of traditional music revival. In Aberdeen, for instance, several informants reported the folk club in the 1960s as having an almost puritanical reverence for traditional music.

In many cases the establishment of new music policies was carried out almost ruthlessly. Ewan MacColl was perhaps the leading figure of this new direction in the folk clubs. MacColl was not antipathetic to American music – far from it, since he married the accomplished American folk singer, Peggy Seeger – but in the Singers' Club he instigated a policy that people should sing only their own national music. At this time not only did American music figure in the folk scene, but many people had taken to singing the music of other countries, Israeli music, Serbo-Croat music and so on, though this music was performed by people who were anything but Israeli, Serbian or Croatian. Almost as a reaction it became policy at the club that only Americans should play American music, only the English sing English songs and so on.

Broadly speaking, two camps emerged, and an insight into what these were like at the time is given by Bob Pegg (1969), one of the leading folk revivalists of the late 1960s:

> If you're interested in finding out what folk clubs are about, try these two simple exercises.
> (i) Take your guitar down to the local traditional club, look innocent and sing Leonard Cohen's 'Suzanne', or perhaps one of the old skiffle favourites . . . It won't take the audience long to react. If it's near the end of the evening and they've had a few jars, they will openly boo and hiss you, even throw halfpennies. If they're a more genteel lot they'll hide their guffaws and titters behind their hands. After you've finished your one song, the man with his finger in his ear, who thinks he's Ewan MacColl, will ask you politely or otherwise (probably otherwise) to step down.
> (ii) Go to your nearest non-traditional club and try them out with an unaccompanied version of one of the more interesting ballads . . . Don't be too surprised when the audience starts to talk, tell jokes, go to fetch drinks, during your performance. After you've finished your one song, the club organiser, who thinks

Ewan MacColl is a man who sings with his finger in his ear, will ask you to step down.

A return to perceived notions of authenticity and national music swept through the clubs and the conflict between the blues/international/American singers and the British traditionalists formed a tension, if not a schism, in the folk movement. This had two effects. One was the aforementioned division into two types of folk club, the other was the generation of an enormous amount of introspective examination of artistic direction.

The turn towards the native folk tradition did not occur by gradual evolution or 'artistic drift', but was seized upon swiftly and self-consciously. In the folk magazines and newssheets which sprang up, questions of artistic direction and purpose dominated the pages. Editorials, articles, interviews and correspondence presented the views of folk adherents engaged in the construction of a new musical genre. In this material can be found first-hand accounts of the evolution of the folk movement. The ideological and artistic positions struck during the early 1960s have formed the basis for the folk scene and are still represented in the folk clubs of today.

A concern was expressed in folk magazines such as *Ethnic* that many of the early collectors had not done justice to their material. The revival of interest in traditional music in the folk revival was characterised by a desire to seek out traditional 'source' singers. Most of the first generation of professional folk singers touring the folk clubs made contact with traditional singers who had been 'discovered'. In this way source singers such as the Copper Family, Fred Jordan and Jeannie Robertson were embraced by the folk scene and many went on to become 'stars' within it.

Unlike the first generation of collectors who had been concerned with text and melody, much attention was focused on the style of singing traditional song. Sharp had collected songs such as 'The Seeds of Love' and arranged them for pianoforte and the drawing room, causing John England, from whom the song was collected, to remark that this was the first time he had the heard the song performed 'in evening dress'. But in this second 'revival' there was a very different approach to the song material. Peter Bellamy, a professional singer, was typical of this generation of English revivalists:

I was into skiffle, rock 'n' roll, American music. At eighteen I went to art school and I performed black American music and then I discovered the English revival. In '62 Norfolk was rich in source singers and I turned my attention that way. My vocal mannerisms and the things that go to make up what is a pretty distinctive style now are almost entirely based on traditional musicians ... I'm not adhering to any rules, there's no way I could do – or any point in slavishly copying one particular style. I'm not alone in this – look at somebody like Paul Brady. He's probably the best practitioner of the job that I try to do, which is to take traditional songs and above all traditional style in singing them and yet adapt it to make it something relevant and entertaining to today's audience, while still having the important elements of traditional musicianship. That's something I resent in other people working in this field who are simply learning the songs but paying no attention whatsoever to traditional style – style is as important to me as song content and melody, and I think that people who are learning the songs to do them 'their way' may be valid but they're missing at least 50 per cent of the point.

Bellamy's approach highlights certain features of the revival. For a start, the singing of traditional material was not entered into as an escapist return to the past or in the form of historical reproduction. It was quite different from, say, the Sealed Knot in re-enacting battles in authentic reproductions of dress and weapons, or in the way a group of classical musicians may 'authentically' play a medieval piece of music on exact replicas of the instruments of the period.

People such as Bellamy were consciously attempting to develop the music in such a way that it becomes appropriate to use the verb 'evolve' transitively. The aim was not to take this music from one context and transform it in order to impose it on a new context as did Sharp (even though it can be argued that this is precisely what they did do!). Bellamy went to 'source' singers, that is to say, living traditional exponents of the music, avoiding some of the 'mediations' which characterise Harker's (1985) criticism of notions of authenticity in English folk song.

For many in the folk scene, 'authentic' reproduction of old songs was less important than establishing a link with the past to establish continuity:

> Since the early days of the 'broadside ballads' and before, men and women have been making songs about their lives, just for the sheer joy of expressing feelings which they couldn't express in ordinary conversation. It is therefore vital that all clubs gatherings should LIVE, that is that they should do three things.
> (1) GET PEOPLE SINGING
> (2) GIVE INFORMATION ON THE SONGS AND THE SINGERS, in order to rekindle a fresh, living tradition.
> (3) USE ANY PROFITS TO BRING SINGERS INTO THE CLUBS, who would not normally be heard by the club members (*Spin*, vol. 1, no. 2, November 1961).

The focus of attention was not an entity, 'the song', but a process, 'get people singing'. The aim was not to reconstruct the past from its songs and music but to change the social role of music from one where music-making was in the hands of the music industry to one where the control of music-making was restored to ordinary people. This may have been far more important to the symbolic role of the revival of traditional song than the actual song texts and melodies themselves – and if this was the case, the fact that 'mediations' of texts had occurred might not be particularly relevant to the ideological role of the modern folk scene. This point emerges strongly from Peter Bellamy's comments above. It is not so much the songs themselves but their style which he concentrates on and it is this which he sees as the most important facet of 'traditional' singing for the revivalist.

But it is also important to note that the folk scene did, right from the beginning, function through the cash nexus. From very early on there were folk professionals who made a living through folk singing, and others who made a living out of the folk scene through their work in record companies, or as concert promoters and so on. The ultra-purist phase of the traditional clubs also did not last long. Myra Abbott, for instance, mentions that she soon softened her approach but affirms that this attitude had been necessary to establish not just the traditional repertoire but also traditional styles of singing in the clubs. The central ground shifted to one of deep consideration of the conflict between tradition and innovation in the clubs.

Albert Lloyd (1962), an influential commentator on the folk club movement, put it like this:

> The argument rages in the folk clubs; how much should tradition be respected, to what extent is innovation welcome? In a way it's the central problem of the current folk song revival.
> Cecil Sharp . . . saw that the process by which a folk song is created and performed is governed by three factors: continuity which links the present with the past; variation which springs from the creative impulse of the individual; selection by the community which determines the form in which the piece survives.
> In other words to be satisfactory and memorable to the community a folk song must be founded on certain inflexible principles, but subjected constantly to individual treatment. Implicit in Sharp's formulation is the vital dialectic of folk song creation, the perpetual struggle for synthesis between collective taste and individual fancy, between what has gone before and what is needed now, between tradition and innovation.

In the article Lloyd articulates ways in which he feels the dialogue between tradition and innovation should be attempted in the context of the revival:

> by all means try new ways of performing folk songs; but familiarise yourself too with what's best in the old ways. Then be sure that in applying your new treatment, you're not discarding something that was valuable in the old. Remember, not all folk songs need new treatment in order to be viable . . . Respect continuity; be judicious in variation; be generous in selection.

This advice was taken to heart and characterised the attitude of the majority of revival performers, for instance as typified by Bellamy. Whether people did follow Lloyd's advice or whether Lloyd was only expressing a common feeling that was sweeping through the folk movement is unclear. Nevertheless Lloyd, along with a few others such as Ewan MacColl, was very self-conscious with regard to the nature of 'tradition' and 'revival'. Lloyd has repeated these views in at least a score of similar articles in folk magazines.

Perhaps the most remarkable facet of this process is the way in which 'academic' discussion and examination of the nature of tradition, especially through the writings of Sharp and Lloyd, were taken up as models for artistic praxis. Lloyd's article had not been written for an academic conference but for singers and musicians, the very singers and musicians who were taking to this traditional body of material with such enthusiasm. Perceived notions of tradition, traditionality, and of the function of artistic innovation in 'traditional' contexts were self-consciously held up as models for dealing with and relating to the corpus of traditional song and music. Article after article in the early years dealt with notions of artistic direction, the role of traditional song in the revival, and social, political, musical and cultural objectives. For instance, an editorial in *Ethnic* (vol. 1, no. 2, Spring 1959) said: 'Behind this discussion lies the very important question of what we in the Revival are in relation to the live tradition.'

Bell (1963) laid out some grandiose plans:

> The enormous increase in the number of folk clubs is heart-warming but by its nature very limited. People who know and love folk music and dancing are in effect setting up little chapels where they can meet and pray, and different and warring sects are emerging. Meanwhile what about the unconverted? Shouldn't we be preaching on the street corners to those who've never heard the gospels? The kids are still spending £8 or £9 million a year on pops and being denied the chance to create their own culture because they don't know...What's the answer? For a start let's stop quarrelling among ourselves about the sacred nature of our folk culture. We need more than a revival – we need the beginning of a new culture and that culture must be based on the present day, not on a mythical golden age.

Sometimes even the self-consciousness appeared self-conscious, as in the following editorial (*Ethnic*, vol. 1, no. 3, Summer 1959):

> It is against the laws of nature that people should be able to play and sing as part of the living tradition and at the same time be able to conduct rational polemics...but we are thankful to say that an increasing number of people are acquiring these incompatible abilities.

And these polemics were taking place throughout Britain in magazines, folk festivals and clubs. In 1964 the English Folk Dance and Song Society held a festival at Keele to which many exponents of traditional song were invited. Clubs started to book guests more frequently, sparking a generation of professional folk performers. And throughout the 1960s a host of performers took to the folk scene, some traditionally orientated and others writing their own material. But by the mid-1960s the flirtation of folk with the popular music of the day which had occurred with skiffle was over, at least to the extent that, to the alarm of the music industry, it had been prophesied that it might become the new popular music.

The next chapters will now be concerned with what became of this revival, because, while no longer at the forefront of popular culture after the mid-1960s, it by no means vanished. Chapter 4 will provide a brief description of the folk club scene of the late 1980s, and we will then turn to the analysis of social and musical dynamics.

4   Folk Clubs in Great Britain

The folk scene today is far from homogeneous. Attempting to pin it down is not helped by the wider currency of the term 'folk' in music, wider certainly than regular attenders of events in the folk scene would prefer, for instance its use to refer to some pub 'folk nights'. In addition, there is the more recent problem that a section of the folk scene is tending to drop the term 'folk', perhaps because of this wider currency, in favour of descriptive labels such as 'roots music', 'ethnic music', 'traditional music' or even the absence of a label altogether, as in the case of some folk festivals which now simply call themselves 'festivals'. However, folk is no different from other musical genres in that different perceptions of the music are held by those not involved or interested compared to those of aficionados. This gulf may be wider for folk music, because it has a very low profile in the mass media. Those who do not attend folk scene events are unlikely to come into contact with folk music except from prior contact during its heyday in the early 1960s, from school, or if they happen to be in a town during a folk festival.

Within the folk scene there are a range of organisational forms. The music is performed in folk clubs, folk festivals, sessions, singarounds, dances, ceilidhs, concerts, the street, pub rooms, private parties and so on. Within these categories, for instance the folk clubs, it is possible to go further and identify specific sub-classes of event. In nearly all areas of Britain there is a local folk magazine with details of clubs and folk events, and small editorial sections and articles. In addition, there is an English *Folk Directory* and a *Scottish Folk Directory* listing clubs, artists, organisations and other reference material relating to the folk scene.

There is a roughly even distribution of folk clubs over Britain as a whole: thus the 1986 *Folk Directory* (Dowell 1985) lists 12 folk clubs in the West Midlands and 28 in Yorkshire, and the *Scottish Folk Directory* of the same year (Douglas 1986) lists 22 clubs. Overall these two sources list 468 clubs in Great Britain. This is probably an underestimate: some clubs fail to provide details for the directories and, although the compilers endeavour to track these down, some are missed out; in addition, few singaround clubs (clubs which do not book guest artists) are listed; and every folk agency I contacted reported the existence of a larger number of clubs than officially listed. For instance, Acorn Entertainments, a folk agency which acts a sole agent for several of the 'top' names on the folk scene, was dealing (in 1987) with 864 folk clubs. This was the number of folk clubs throughout Great Britain into which they could book artists. These are all artists who are at the top of the fee range which might exclude many smaller clubs, though many quite small clubs will occasionally splash out on one of these artists. The manager of Acorn Entertainments mentioned one club with an average attendance of only 24 per week which saves up and books Martin Carthy 'as a treat'. It is also interesting to note that Acorn records an expansion in the number of folk clubs over the last few years. In 1978 Acorn listed just over 500 clubs.

A survey of folk clubs in one region, 'Folk Music in East Anglia' (Atterson 1984) gives a quantitative indication of the structure of the folk club movement. This survey was compiled as a submission to the East Anglian Arts Association Music Panel. A questionnaire survey was carried out on all 50 folk clubs in the region which book guests. Replies were received from 24 clubs. The survey indicates a broad similarity across the range of folk clubs in terms of venue, entrance price, presence of 'resident' singers, frequency of meeting and so on. There was more of a spread in terms of the cost of guests, with some clubs concentrating on the bottom of the price range and others on higher-priced guests. A feature which should be noted is that, along with the existence of long-standing clubs, there is also some 'regeneration' occurring. New folk clubs are still being formed. On the basis of the survey the report presents a picture of a typical folk club:

> Held in the club room of a pub, it has been going for nearly 20 years. Meetings are held weekly throughout the year, from 8 until 11.00 p.m. The landlord is quite cooperative, provided the audience have a few drinks; he charges a minimum rent, to cover heating and cleaning, and he arranges two or three late licences per year for special evenings. The room can hold just over 100 but is usually about half full, except on special guest nights (about six per year), when capacity is often reached before 8.30 p.m., and the door must be closed.
>
> Professional guests are booked three times a month, with singarounds on the other nights(s); the average cost for a guest is about £60 [in 1984] but is tending upwards all the time, usually because of travel expenses. Annual membership is open to all who comply with the licensing laws, and costs £1–50 per annum. On normal nights, members are entitled to a 20 pence reduction, and they are given priority on tickets for the big name nights; only very occasionally is the admission price increased, for particularly expensive guests. The club has a mutual relationship with three other local clubs.
>
> Admission is normally £1–50 for non-members, and £1–30 for members. The average income weekly is £65.
>
> As well as the guest fee, there are other expenses, including entertainment and accommodation of the guest, hire of the room, advertising, printing, and booking expenses especially telephone costs.
>
> There are 8 resident performers, plus another 12 to 15 regulars who are good

for a song or two on singaround nights; most of the latter sing unaccompanied, but the residents play a variety of instruments as well as singing a wide variety of songs. The organiser himself is a singer who features his own songs, but also has a repertoire of several hundred traditional songs and tunes. . . .

(Atterson 1984: 10)

Most folk clubs are run by a committee elected by the membership, though a number of clubs are run by 'benevolent' dictatorships. These committees tend to be organised on standard committee lines, and meet separately from the club night. The Hoy at Anchor folk club, which is fairly typical, has the following committee roles: chairman, treasurer, bookings secretary, minutes secretary, newsletter editor, assistant treasurer, and four people doing publicity (one coordinating, one covering newspapers and magazines, one radio and one doing posters). Committee members divide responsibility between them for the duties that have to be fulfilled on club nights such as compère, door, clearing up, providing accommodation for the guests (normally in their own home) and, though not in this club, the setting up and taking down of the public address system.

The committees assume total control for the week-to-week running of the club, and committee members tend to take their duties seriously. For instance, the current chairman of the Hoy at Anchor folk club, Bryan Martin, commented that:

Much more often than anyone realises, a guest cancels at short notice and the bookings secretary should have enough contacts and enough energy to then spend a day panicking on the telephone. If that happens two weeks in advance it's very difficult to find a replacement. The club should only dimly be aware that there has been a change of programme. Only very rarely, when the guest cancels the day before, does the club become aware that there has been a sudden change.

The duties can come to seem arduous, as one committee member of Aberdeen folk club pointed out:

Sometimes I get totally pissed off with it because you get too much . . . when you are on the committee and you have responsibilities you have to fulfil when you're there.

I attended the committee meetings of Aberdeen folk club for a period of six months. These would take up most of the evening. Club policy and direction were discussed intently at nearly every meeting. A typical committee meeting included discussion on: club lighting and ambience; overall club direction; arrangement of club Burns night; folk club book collection; planning of ceilidh, special guest night, special concert; publicity (posters, press, and club newsletter); accounts; possible future guests to be booked; incentive trials (for people to turn up on time); advance ticket sales for special club nights; club party.

Committees are elected by an annual general meeting which usually occurs on a club night. The club evening is normally given over to a discussion of club policy and is followed by a short singaround. In some clubs the AGM can pass resolutions which are binding upon the committee. However, week to week decisions are normally left to the committee. Membership is open to the general public.

Most clubs are constituted by a formal written constitution which is amendable by the AGM. Committee members are invariably not paid for their duties. The only perk commonly provided is free admission. A small expense allowance would generally be paid to someone who was accommodating a guest – virtually all folk clubs arrange for guests to be accommodated by a committee member or a member of the club. Other expenses, such as the telephone costs of the organiser, would be reimbursed.

For this study I visited over thirty folk clubs, from Inverness to Southampton; I tried to include as many types of club as possible. Although I could not be said to have to have sampled the clubs in any statistically rigorous sense because there is no population census of folk clubs, I attempted to cover the range of club types which I found to exist in given locales, from local information given to me by club attenders, newsletters and so on. I restricted myself to 'folk clubs' which was nevertheless definitionally difficult. These I determined on the basis of clubs which called themselves folk clubs or 'traditional music clubs' or clubs listed in the national or regional folk directories. I noted that there were distinct sub-classes of folk clubs.

The smallest and most informal are the 'singers' clubs'. These are clubs which meet on a regular basis, weekly, fortnightly or monthly, normally in the back room of a pub. They do not book guests and the performers for the night are drawn from whoever happens to turn up. The audience comprises the performers and vice versa. Thus who turns up and who performs is normally left to chance. The evenings are structured with an 'MC' (from 'master of ceremonies', though never referred to as such and frequently female), who announces the start and end of the evening and the intervals, normally one or two. These clubs are sometimes run on such lines because they have fallen on hard times and no longer have the attendances and hence the revenues to be able to book guests. However, many have always run to this format and exist to provide a contrasting type of folk club to others in the area.

An example of such a club is Blackmore folk club in central Essex. This meets weekly in a 400-year-old pub in the small village of Blackmore. The village is largely comprised of buildings of the same period. The club room is up a flight of stairs displaying the typical irregularities of seventeenth-century construction. The room is very small and the chairs are arranged around the walls to leave a vacant space in the middle of the room.

On entering I was immediately welcomed and asked if I was going to contribute to the evening. The entrance money was collected at the door and those who performed were not charged. The entrance fee was in any case only 35p. The club night began with only eight people present, which after about an hour had risen to the night's maximum of 25. People sang and played from their seats. One of the two organisers mentioned to me that they used to have a 'singers' chair' from which people would perform:

> *N*: But it seems to go by the board these days. The organisation's gone to pot but going round the room seems to work.

The evening was very informal. There was an MC who called upon people to sing or play and who announced the beer breaks. There was no bar in the room. People would go down to the bar, as frequently out of a beer break as in one, though not normally while someone was actually singing. The room was lit by the ordinary room lights. The club's two organisers were both in their twenties. I asked them about the organisation of the club.

> *N*: Simon and I take turns to MC. We're appointed because we want to do it. There's no pecking order in the club. If a bunch of singers come along the regulars get missed out. The club is at the disadvantage of having no guests but the atmosphere is unique because it's only audience. We're the only singers' club in the area . . . There's been some bad patches but there's never been so few that we can't do anything. What's disappeared is the audience, not the performers. It's still difficult getting everyone on.

As is indicated here, the folk clubs remained very much an institution whose dominant ethos was performance and participation. Both organisers commented that the club has been maintained by one or two keen devotees who have concentrated their efforts on the club for a few years and then passed on its running to someone else, essentially in the same format. They commented how they had the feeling that they were passing on a heritage:

> *N*: One of the things in taking on a heritage is we can't say we're going to close things. We have ideas but we can't do them. We don't want to lose what it is that we have to offer . . .
> *NLM*: How long has the club been going?
> *S*: Twenty-three years. It's survived because it hasn't changed. I've been put in charge of it if you like. I didn't work my way up the hierarchy to take the club over 'cause the folk scene doesn't work like that. So I've been entrusted with the club. And I'm just going to make sure that it carries on going for the next twenty-three years.

Notions of heritage, tradition and continuity remain strong organising concepts. There is also an awareness that the club is a self-conscious creation:

> *S*: The Blackmore room is a tiny little poky dear old room. It lends itself perfectly to it. You get the impression that folk clubs have been like that all through this century. They haven't as it happens – they've only been going twenty years.

The club, meeting in a tiny historic village, certainly seems a 'natural' setting for a traditionally orientated folk club. But I found the following comment very indicative:

> *NLM*: Does the club have a link with the local community?
> *N*: No. People here come a distance. There are no locals. Its strength is that it's not in a town.

Thus the adherents are searching for a particular 'feeling', one which is deemed appropriate for celebrating 'traditional' music. But folk clubs such as this one are not the venues for local community participation.

Despite the small size of the club and the very informal and relaxed feel of the night, the club nevertheless had a 'tight' structure. There were breaks, but during the performing part of the night the club maintained its cohesiveness and continuity under the steering of the MC. Although it was a 'folk' club with a performance repertoire drawing heavily on the collected (and mediated) material of the English folk tradition, this was not exclusively so. The organisers mentioned that sometimes 'jazz and croony' songs were performed, 'but not rock and pop'. What was appropriate was 'anything slightly not run of the mill'.

From my observation I estimated the age breakdown of the audience as follows:

Age of attenders:	<20	20–29	30–39	40–49	50–59	>60
Percentage of audience:	2	20	20	50	8	0

indicating a very strongly 'middle-aged' dominance.

This club was at one end of a spectrum with regard to scale. Blackmore's annual turnover was only £150.

There is a continuum of clubs from the likes of Blackmore, through those which book a guest a few times each year, those which book guests fortnightly, to a few which book them exclusively, some even with no 'floor' spots whatsoever, though this is unusual. Certainly the most typical folk clubs are those which book guests on a regular basis interspersed with non-guest nights which are billed as 'open' or 'singers'' nights, normally one a month. This covers a wide range of clubs which differ with regard to characteristics of performance repertoire, organisational structure and audience–performer dynamics. The chief differences occur in how 'traditional' the club is, that is, the degree to which the British folk tradition is central in the performance repertoire, as well as the extent to which the paid performer or unpaid performers form the focus of club nights. Performances by local unpaid 'floor' singers on evenings on which there is a booked guest are key features of most folk clubs.

The bulk of the folk clubs are those that book guests interspersed with occasional singers' nights. Musically the clubs range from those wedded to the folk traditions of the British Isles to those embracing blues and stylistically contemporary material. They vary in size from small clubs which book cheaper artists and use singers' nights to cross-subsidise guest nights, to large clubs booking nationally known names virtually every week. There is also variation in what I could only describe as 'cosiness'. The cosiest clubs are those which give the appearance of being a group of friends, with much good-natured banter as the floor singers get up to perform, enthusiastic joining in of choruses, an attentive audience and little background chatter. At the other extreme are clubs which are verging towards weekly concerts. There are clubs which are looking outwards and attracting new audiences and others which are more inward-looking and making no special promotional efforts.

Chelmsford folk club in Essex is an example of a successful, solvent club drawing heavily, though far from exclusively, on the folk tradition. It has been in existence since the early 1960s and is fairly large, with an average attendance of about seventy. On the three evenings I attended this varied from forty to eighty people. It met in British Legion premises in a large rectangular room about seven by fourteen metres. The seating was arranged in oval rows facing the stage. A number of people stood at the back near the door from which there was access to the bar which was outside the room. There was a steady movement of people to the bar during the evening and even during songs, though these movements were nearly always carried out discreetly to give the minimum disruption. The club used public address equipment, although this was not used at any great volume.

Inside the door was a table where the entrance money was collected and a number of people stood about casually in this area for a time during performances. The evening began unannounced when some musicians at the front got out their instruments and started playing. This gave a relaxed feeling to the evening which was then more formally opened by an MC. At this point the chatter subsided and performances were heard in near silence. However, the audience was far from static. There was a general milling about at the back of the room, with people coming in or going out to the bar. A large number of people stood at the back, not for want of seats, which gave to the whole audience an ambience of gentle movement and non-passivity.

In each half there were three floor spots before the guest artists, and I was told that this number would vary slightly from week to week. There was no noise intrusion from outwith the hall and the stage was well lit by bright spotlights. The audience was illuminated with coloured lights and the main hall lighting turned off. The side of the stage was blocked off by curtains. Folk club posters advertising other events were posted around the room. The room was in a good state of décor and gave a comfortable if not an extravagant feel. The MC did not speak for long when announcing performers, a business which he attended to in a very informal way. The audience was dressed casually. Its age structure was very similar to that of Blackmore, but with a slightly higher representation of younger age groups. Older persons of retirement age were again entirely absent. The club is run by a committee, though one of the organisers informed me that:

> It's a sort of very loose committee. Everyone's got their little job and they get on with it.

It was commented that a general change had come over the club which was also true of the folk scene in general:

> S: The role of the folk club has changed dramatically over the past ten years. It used to be you went into the backstairs room of a pub and you got together and you sang songs and that was it . . . There was no playing to the general public. It was a very insular thing. But now in this area you've got two Morris sides dancing during the week. We've got three sessions in pubs and three to four nights of the week you can go out and get free music and free singing in pubs not very far away, so if you are going to start charging people to come in and see something it's got to be an appreciably better standard.

The club now meets in the local British Legion club because of the problems of finding suitable premises, a point mentioned by several folk club organisers. For a while the club met in a night club but there was a general feeling that the décor of a disco unit was not conducive to a folk club atmosphere.

The club nights are meticulously organised, though it is up to the MC on the night which floor artists will be put on. But this differs on a non-guest night, which here they call a 'club night':

> We just go along with nothing planned. No seats out and we just get on with it. And it gives everyone a chance to have a chat, have a dance and try and join in the band. We tend not to get so many of the general public in on those nights.

On the three evenings I attended this club there were three very different types of guest: a singer/songwriter comedian, a duo who played traditional Irish music; and a modern revival instrumental band playing music from continental Europe arranged in an upbeat manner.

There was a striking difference in presentation between guests and floor singers, with the latter being less overtly direct, tending to get on with their musical performance without much introduction. Nevertheless, there were some extremely talented and proficient singers and musicians among the floor singers, interspersed with one or two who were lacking in ability and/or confidence. One girl in particular looked so stage-struck that she was scarcely able to complete her performance. When I commented on this to one of the organisers I realised from his reply that he had scarcely considered this as a flaw to an evening which he thought to be 'excellent'. It occurred to me that there was a tolerance of differing standards, indeed on this occasion the audience showed no sign of dissatisfaction, and sang her choruses with greater verve than for other more accomplished floor singers.

I would describe this club as being within the middle range of successful clubs. I came across some clubs that concentrated upon more traditional artists and some that were particularly 'cosy'. I took this term both from the organisers' own description and from my own impressions deriving from such factors as the amount of performer–audience interaction, absence of background chatter, whether I was spoken to when I had not previously introduced myself, and so on. One particularly revealing gauge I came to adopt in identifying cosiness was the distance of the performer to the nearest member of the audience. Most folk clubs, except those veering to the concert format, attempt to minimise this. In the case of Chelmsford the distance was two metres but in other clubs it could be even less than one, with the crossed legs of the frontmost person nearly touching the performer.

Lindon folk club, Northumberland, was a club at another extreme of the folk club spectrum, being in effect a regular concert since it did not have floor singers. The club meets monthly and always books a main guest and a support act. But I would still consider it a folk club for several reasons: first, it describes itself as such; second, it is run by people experienced in running folk clubs and follows the format of folk clubs right down to the 'parish notices', a term used by folk clubs themselves when the MC announces what other folk activities are going on in the area that week; third, the club exuded a 'cosy' feeling reminiscent of folk clubs in general; and fourth, though there were no floor spots the organisers always engaged a group or performer as a support act who were local, effectively taking the place of floor singers.

The club was organised in a formal manner but had a friendly atmosphere – for instance, there was some good-natured heckling and guests and audience mingled at the start. It met in a medium-sized oblong room with an oval seating arrangement with the guests performing from a stage along one side. It was housed in a very stylish period hotel. I estimated the age structure of the audience as follows:

Age of attenders:	<20	20–29	30–39	40–49	50–59	>60
Percentage attending:	10	50	15	15	10	0

This indicates a dominance of the 20–29 age group, with again no representation of those aged over 60.

The stage was clearly marked off and separate from the audience who filled the room. The main guest was a virtuosic guitarist and consummately professional performer. His performance was heard in rapt attention with a certain air of admiration. This night was a good example of how the folk scene can present a polished appearance, though I should add that this was often true of many of the more 'cosy' clubs as well. At most clubs, the quality of the floor singers is an important factor, but one which added elements of unpredictability both to musical content and to the 'polish' of any given night. At Lindon the organisers spoke disapprovingly about this effect of floor spots on guest nights:

> Some people can control it but many clubs can't. You get a big section of people who've always been involved with the club who play, who expect to get onto the stage every time the club's on and sing – usually the same songs that they've sung for years and years. I've always found it a considerable embarrassment to sit and watch them and often the people who they were paying their money to see didn't really get a chance. I've seen the guest going on for the last ten minutes which is what we wanted to avoid. We got stick at the beginning with people coming with guitars but it's just our way.

The club was set up in 1982. Several of the clubs I visited had started up recently and this is an important point to note given how often folk club organisers are prepared to sound off about the impending demise of the folk scene.

Musical performance in each of these folk clubs is tightly structured. We have seen how historical feel can be important and how the scale of the venue and the social dynamics are given careful consideration. Later in this book I will probe these themes analytically, but before doing so I will examine the tastes and characteristics of folk club audiences.

5   The Folk Club Audience Survey

Introduction

A questionnaire was administered to a national sample of folk club attenders in the winter of 1986–7. First, I wanted to discover something about the identity of the folk club audience. Who are the folkies? So questions were asked to ascertain the demography and socio-economic profile of folk club attenders. Second, I wanted to find out about the general attitudes and dispositions of folk club attenders. Did they have a distinctive dispositional and attitude profile? Finally, it was important to know what the audience thought about folk music and the extent of attenders' participation and involvement.

A sample of ten clubs was chosen, extending from Edinburgh to Southampton, and including clubs in London, Birmingham, Sheffield, Newcastle upon Tyne, and rural clubs in Essex, Northumberland, Yorkshire and Strathclyde. They were selected to encompass a wide geographical spread and folk club type. They ranged from clubs which had been going thirty years to one which was a year old, from clubs with an audience of a dozen to one with an audience of over a hundred, from posh suburbs to a pit village. The entire audience on a given club night was handed a questionnaire which was to be returned by post.

A tabular breakdown of some of the results discussed in this chapter is presented in the appendix. A fuller version is presented in my PhD thesis (MacKinnon 1988). Five hundred questionnaires were issued of which 284 were returned, a rate of return of 57 per cent. All differences referred to in the text between the sample and national population are significant at the 95 per cent level and most are significant at the 99 per cent level.

Who are the folkies?

The division of the sample by gender was 59 per cent male and 41 per cent female. The age distribution of the sample (Table 1 in Appendix) was skewed, with very few teenagers, a quarter of the sample in the 30–34 age group, nearly half in the 30–39 age group and very few in the older age groups. It therefore appears that folk clubs are not appealing to those in their early twenties or younger, nor to the over-sixties.

I was intrigued by the presence of such a bulge in the distribution for 30–45-year-olds. Could this be due to the presence of a large group of people who had come across this music in its heyday and maintained their musical loyalty, or were people were still being drawn in on a large scale today? Have the same people stayed with the folk club movement and grown older with it? Or is the folk club movement actively drawing in new adherents? Thus, is the bulge itself static or moving 'down' the population pyramid? This point is of some significance for the viability of the scene.

Some questions were inserted into the questionnaire to test this. Respondents were asked their current age and the date of first attendance at a folk club. This provided strong evidence of the origins of the folk club movement as a youth sub-culture (Table 2 in Appendix). Nearly half the sample first attended before the age of 20. But what is remarkable is that there is an almost complete absence of this age group in today's audience. Further analysis of the data also indicated that the folk club movement did continue as a youth culture well after its heyday in the 1960s. By splitting the sample into age cohorts I was able to examine in which years teenagers were being drawn into the folk scene and found that this age group continued to be drawn in up to the early 1980s. Only in the current audience profile do teenagers vanish. The data indicate that there has been a rupture very recently, which would correspond to what Smith has termed 'The Folk Doom of the 80's' (Smith 1986). The folk scene thus appears to be an ageing movement, but is this evidence of its impending demise? Further analysis indicated that the folk club movement is continuing to attract new attenders; a fifth of the current audience, as indicated by this sample, were drawn in during the period 1980–7, but these people tended to be older. The demographic profile does not indicate that the folk scene is necessarily in danger of disappearing, but does point to its appeal being no longer that of a youth sub-culture.

I will now turn to an examination of the socio-economic profile of the sample. Respondents were asked to record their occupation. These were subsequently categorised according to the Registrar General's categorisations of social class (Table 3 in Appendix).

The sample was heavily weighted towards the upper social classes, with a much higher representation of social class II (intermediate non-manual occupations) in particular than the general population. If classes I and II are grouped together then these comprise 62 per cent of the folk club audience, compared to 28 per cent of the general population. There was also a very low representation of manual workers, comprising 60 per cent of the general population but only 18 per cent of the folk club sample, and virtually all of these were contained within the skilled manual category, social class III(M).

The sample was also examined according to the Registrar General's classification of socio-economic group (Table 4 in Appendix). It is derived from occupation and employment status but its function is different from social class, being more refined and concentrating upon status, aiming to group together jobs of similar social and economic status.

Here a pattern emerged beyond that apparent from the data on social class. It is not simply the case that the higher occupational groupings are better represented in folk clubs because, from the data on socio-economic group, employers and managers (SG 1) are not substantially differently represented from the general population. However, professional workers (SGs 3 and 4) are considerably over-represented and those in socio-economic group 5.1 overwhelmingly so, comprising well over a third of the total sample. This is the grouping representing occupations ancillary to the professions, but not necessarily requiring education to university degree standard, such as teachers and librarians.

The breakdown by highest educational qualification achieved showed a striking difference to the general population (Table 5 in Appendix). The differences here were even greater than for occupational classifications. The sample indicated very high levels of formal education. Over a third had degrees, compared to 8 per cent nationally. Seventy-five per cent of the folk club sample were educated to A-level equivalent or higher, compared to a Great Britain figure of 25 per cent. While 46 per cent of the national population had no qualifications at all, this only applied to 11 per cent of the folk club sample.

I had also included questions which allowed an examination of social mobility in direct comparison to the national sample of the *General Household Survey*. On a simple index of upward, static or downward social mobility from one generation to the next, 52 per cent of the sample were found to be upwardly mobile compared to 14 per cent of the general population (Table 6 in Appendix). This is a particularly revealing item of information relating to the social structure of the folk club audience. Not only were folk club attenders weighted towards specific sections of the higher socio-economic groups but their inter-generational social class trajectory is upward, and markedly more so than for the population as a whole.

The audience: General attitudes and dispositions

A section of the questionnaire had been constructed to probe extra-musical factors which might associate with support for folk music. It was concerned with the tastes, dispositions, general opinions and consumption patterns of the sample and their comparison with the general public.

An overall leisure profile for the sample was constructed from a question asking respondents which listed activities and pursuits they had taken part in or gone to in the previous four weeks (Table 7 in Appendix). This question was directly drawn from the *General Household Survey* and hence again provided direct comparison with the national population. I regarded it as a 'strong' question because it asked directly about the respondents' pattern of activity within a specified time period.

Sex, socio-economic group and age were controlled for in order to ascertain those differences which were not just due to the extremely atypical profile of the sample. For nearly every selected leisure activity the level of participation of folk club attenders was substantially higher than for the national sample. Only for gardening and darts was it lower and even then only very slightly. Listening to records and tapes during the previous month was a nearly unanimous activity, compared to a participation of 63 per cent for the general public in the previous four weeks (Office of Population Censuses and Surveys 1983a).

'Going out for a drink and a meal' evidenced a higher rate for the folk club sample than the national sample in all sub-categories. It is interesting to note that the difference with regard to having 'gone out for a drink' among the national sample varies by sex: 46 per cent female as against 64 per cent male, but hardly at all for the folk club sample, 88 per cent female as against 86 per cent male. Activities which displayed participation rates very much higher than for the national sample were visits to the 'theatre/opera/ballet', to historic buildings and to museums and art galleries. These activities also associate with socio-economic class. However, while the direction of difference with regard to social class was the same for both the folk club and national samples with the higher socio-economic classes evidencing the higher participation rates, it was the case that when social class was allowed for, there were still stark differences between the two samples. Thus the participation rate for 'visiting a historic building or town' for the general public was 8 per cent overall rising to 13 per cent in the professional, managerial and intermediate grouping, compared to 32 per cent and 42 per cent, respectively, for the folk club sample. For 'theatre/opera/ballet' it was 4 per cent rising to 9 per cent, and 35 per cent rising to 44 per cent, respectively, for each sample; and, for museum/art gallery attendance, 3 per cent and 5 per cent, and 25 per cent and 33 per cent, respectively. Thus the differences cannot be accounted for by the highly atypical socio-economic grouping of the folk club sample.

This examination of participation rates in selected leisure activities indicates that the typical folk club goer is quite different from the public at large. The overall impression of the folk club sample compared to the general population is of a group that is especially active, erudite, aesthetically and artistically orientated.

A comparable question was also inserted on attitudes to diet and health. The rationale was as follows. For many groups in Britain health has become a fad. There has been a tendency towards 'health consciousness' in recent years – vegetarianism, reduction in levels of smoking, reducing fat intake and so on. Such attitudes are particularly prevalent among those referred to as 'the muesli left'. Are the folkies a sub-set of the muesli left? Is support for folk and traditional music a part of the same constellation of consciousness that embraces a concern for healthy living? Across a range of activities the folk club audience evidenced a far higher frequency of participation in activities which are specifically undertaken in order to keep well and healthy (Table 8 in Appendix). This was especially the case with regard to 'eating properly'. In mentioning the muesli left, the 'muesli' element would certainly seem to apply. Whether the 'left' element applies is more relevant to the next section of questions.

Voting intention at a general election indicated a more left-wing orientation (Table 9 in Appendix). To the question 'Do you think British society deliberately excludes some kinds of people from a chance to make a good living, or does everyone have a chance?' the folk club audience was much less supportive of the proposition that 'everyone has a chance' (32 per cent) than the general population (53 per cent) (Gallup 1984b). As an indicator which would differentiate the muesli left from those on the left generally, concern for the environment is perhaps paramount and a higher level of concern was indicated by the folk club audience than for a national sample.

Church attendance of folk club attenders was much lower. Over three-quarters (76 per cent) stated they never attend, compared to less than half (46 per cent) of the British sample (Neuhaus 1986). This may be quite an indicative finding. In many ways the folk club movement has features in common with a church, or perhaps more precisely a non-conformist meeting house. Folk club attenders usually attend the same folk club on a weekly basis. The folk club involves attenders as active participants. Attenders take part in communal music-making. Could it be that lower church attendance among folk club attenders could be accounted for by the fact that a folk club discharges many of the same functions as a church? This is a line of enquiry that might be interesting to pursue for other types of organisation that greatly involve their participants, whether secular or religious.

The question 'Do you have an autobank card?' may at first sight appear to be a strange one to have included, but I will show why I feel its results to be quite revealing. The folk scene draws upon many historical referents. I wondered whether respondents themselves had an attachment to the past which could be described as romantic or nostalgic; whether there was a resistance to innovation; or whether the articulation of this relationship was more complicated. Certainly if this audience were in some way directly resisting the modern world then we would expect to see this resistance evidenced in certain patterns of non-musical behaviour. I selected possession of an autobank card because I considered this typical of a modern innovation which is quite recent and hence highly innovatory, and yet has become widespread in a short period. As an innovation it is both 'high tech' and also recasts social relationships within its domain, removing the face-to-face encounter of withdrawing cash. If the 'nostalgia' or 'resistance to modernism' thesis were to hold then I would expect to see some resistance to the embracing of autobank cashcards within the sample. Thus this question could be deemed to be investigating the 'innovatory disposition' of folk club attenders.

The findings indicate rejection of the 'resistance to modernism' hypothesis since possession of an autobank card is far higher at 72 per cent within the sample than for the general population (46 per cent) (Gallup 1986). Certainly on this limited evidence a simple thesis that folk club attenders can be described generally as 'looking back' does not fit.

Finally, an attitudinal question was asked concerning general well-being and the folk club sample were found to be decisively more dissatisfied than the general public. The questionnaire does not indicate why, but given much higher levels of participation in leisure pursuits it cannot be because they do not have enough to do. Neither is it because they are in financial difficulties or in low-grade jobs.

The audience and its music

By the time I analysed the audience questionnaire I had formed many hypotheses and hunches as to audience structure and identity. But were my interpretations, based on observations and qualitative interviews, representative? I came to see this as a valuable aspect of the study. Not only would the survey give an attitudinal and social breakdown of a folk audience, it would also act as a pointer to the qualitative core of the study. In this section I will present the results of the musically orientated questions.

I investigated how frequently members of the folk club audience attended folk-related activities and found that the audience at a folk club was not a transient one. Over half attend most weeks and nearly three-quarters are regular attenders, defined as turning up once a month or more. A folk club thus operates differently from many other musical venues where the audience varies greatly. A third of the sample are also regular attenders of another folk club. Only 11 per cent never go to another folk club, which indicates that, despite high levels of attendance loyalty at one club, there are still considerable cross-overs of attendance with other clubs.

There are substantial levels of attendance at folk-related activities. Respondents were asked their frequency of attendance at: Morris and clog dancing events; dances/ceilidhs; singarounds/sessions; parties where folk music is sung or played; folk concerts; and folk festivals. Non- and virtual non-attenders, being those who never attend any of these events or attend less than a few times each year, comprise only 9 per cent of the sample. Over half, 53 per cent, regularly attend at least one such activity, defined as once a month on average. Nearly three-quarters of the sample attend at least one folk festival per year.

Questions designed to elicit levels of active musical involvement were also included. These are high: 60 per cent sing or play a musical instrument; 42 per cent perform at the folk club they attend. This is as an extremely high level of performance on the part of ordinary attenders at musical events, and I would doubt whether it is matched by many other musical forms in modern Britain.

If we turn now to chorus singing, itself a form of active musical engagement, this encompasses 93 per cent of the audience. Thus fewer than one in ten of the audience are not to some degree actively involved musically. Put another way, only 7 per cent of the sample could be described as 'audience', in the sense of being passive receptors of the artistic efforts of other people. Nevertheless, despite being such a participatory genre, folk club attenders still like to listen to folk music on records and tapes (Table 10 in Appendix). I had asked this question to ascertain whether there was a resistance to the concept of folk music in recorded form, but it appears not.

For over a quarter (29 per cent) of the sample, folk music also comprised the 'main part' of their social life and for nearly three-quarters (72 per cent) a 'large part' of their social life. Nearly half (48 per cent) professed a 'deep interest' in the music, compared to only 17 per cent who stated they came 'mainly for the entertainment' (Table 11 in Appendix). Thus so far the survey has revealed high levels of active musical involvement, of attendance at folk-related activities, of professed deep interest and of social involvement.

Another series of questions sought to ascertain respondents' views and expectations of musical content. Access to the performing platform is readily given in a folk club. A wide range of performers of various types of music are given access, but this does not necessarily mean that the audience approves of their performance in a folk club. Furthermore, there is much argument as to the definition of folk music. Whereas this could be settled practically by looking at what is performed in folk clubs, I decided to ask folk club attenders what types of music they considered 'belong or have their place in a folk club' (Table 12 in Appendix). Certainly a reverence for the folk tradition comes over. I had wondered whether for many the folk clubs might no longer function as a venue for 'source' traditional music. But this is not the case. Ninety-eight per cent agreed that 'singers from the tradition' 'had their place' in a folk club. Blues comes out highly, perhaps surprisingly given its low score for record and tape listening. Modern rock, modern jazz and classically trained singing showed the lowest ratings. But no musical form is considered by less than 10 per cent to be suitable. Around a quarter think that some jazz and rock music has its place. Interestingly, it is the categories of ' "trad" jazz' and '50's and 60's rock and roll' which gain the higher ratings over their modern equivalents. This led me to wonder whether a folk club may operate in some way as an outlet for musical nostalgia.

I wanted to assess respondents' views on the way the folk scene organised itself and on the audience's attitudes to performance. I had noticed that new performers were generally made readily welcome at folk clubs and given a platform. But was this the audience's preference? There was strong agreement to the statement that 'the folk club is very encouraging to new performers'. Seventy per cent agreed that 'the folk club is a good place to make new friends' (with 19 per cent undecided and 11 per cent disagreeing). Exactly the same proportions agreed and disagreed to the proposition that 'On the whole folk music events are run efficiently'.

I was particularly interested to look at the responses to the statement that

'Successful folk performers try hard to remain approachable'. An impression of approachability is given by many folk performers, and the lack of stage doors, dressing rooms and so on adds to this. But was this the audience's perception, or could it be that a section of the audience might 'see through' such devices? If this were the case then a wide disparity in results might appear. I was thus interested to find that 80 per cent of the audience agreed with the statement that 'successful folk performers try hard to remain approachable' while only 6 per cent disagreed.

A question asking for agreement or disagreement as to whether 'the folk scene is an important link with our own past' was included to test a specific hypothesis. Since the folk scene draws from antecedents in the past and celebrates these associations in its music, I wanted to know whether the audience had this link in mind with regard to the musical performance. The sorts of issue that I was interested in included the following. Was the appeal of folk music chiefly a certain organisation of musical sound or was there a wider link? Was the music doing something for a folk audience other than providing musical enjoyment? Was the link with the past contained in the songs themselves something that the audience directly relates to and identifies with? Support for the proposition was very strong, with 89 per cent agreeing and only 5 per cent disagreeing. Thus my hunch that the role of the past is something that a folk audience is identifying with does seem to be valid.

Amplification is an issue which arouses strongly contrasting views in the folk scene. Roughly a third (30 per cent) claimed that public address (PA) systems did enhance their enjoyment of the clubs, 23 per cent were undecided, while nearly a half (47 per cent) rejected this proposition. The antipathy to PA seems high, given the prevalence of PA in most other musical events, with the exception of classical music. However, classical music had already evolved to enable the enlargement or massification of musical performance through the use of large numbers of instruments in the orchestra, through the use of special vocal techniques, acoustically suitable venues and by usually insisting upon absolute silence. These do not apply to the average folk club and make such a large proportion indicating disdain for the use of PA quite remarkable. Views on use of PA showed no tendency to associate with 'level of expressed interest in folk music'. Thus it seems that the folk club attenders are well and truly split on this issue.

Another prevailing issue is that of the standard of performance of the floor performers. From my observations and judgement, poor performing standards are quite prevalent. This is true even at the most basic level of forgetting words and making mistakes, as well as a lack of overt attention to presentation on the part of floor performers. Such an assessment is contained in the replies to a question asking for views on selected propositions about the standard of floor performers (Table 13 in Appendix). Only 12 per cent thought 'There is nothing wrong with the general standard of floor performers'. But of the remainder I find the breakdown most remarkable. Half take the view that 'Variations in standards are healthy being the only way that new performers can gain experience'. This ties in directly with the very high level of support for the proposition that 'The folk club is very encouraging to new performers'.

Even among those who think there should be some effort to raise standards, the reply that was most opted for was the one stating that efforts to improve standards 'should be approached carefully and not be over-emphasised'. Thus what I find remarkable is that while only 12 per cent of the sample claim that there is nothing wrong with the standards of floor performers – the implication being that the remaining 88 per cent do to some extent – only 3 per cent agree with the straightforward proposition that 'The folk club should ensure much higher standards of performance from floor performers'.

The survey has given some indication of the identity, views and disposition of folk club attenders. It has helped in answering questions such as the following. What is it about folk music which attracts certain distinct types of individual? How do the tastes, dispositions and socio-economic background of these individuals shape the development of the folk scene?

The remainder of this book now concerns itself with examining the internal processes of performance in the folk scene.

6 Musical Socialisation

Paths of entrance to performance

The pattern of entry to folk music performance is informal in the sense of occurring largely outwith formalised tuition. Formal lessons in folk music are rare. A very large number of respondents described how they 'happened upon' the folk scene. A floor singer at the Hoy and Anchor folk club who first became involved in 1968 tells of his first involvement:

> *P*: I used to be a member of the yacht club and we used to go out for a drink and we went to a pub in Billericay and there was a lot of people going through to the back room and I thought what's going on there – a disco or a dance? And they said no it's a folk club. And I thought 'Oh finger in the ear job' – so I thought I've never been to one. So we went in and I really loved it.

The chief characteristic of introduction to the folk scene was informality. I did not come across a single case where parents had aspirations for their child to become a folk performer, even when parents were heavily 'into' traditional music. When interest in folk music did span two generations the fact that the next generation took an interest usually appeared accidental. A general pattern was of the folk scene as something 'stumbled across'. Often, as for the floor singer cited above, an impression of folk music had been formed prior to active involvement, which did not correspond to what was found.

The folk scene in the 1960s had a high profile in the media, compared to the almost complete lack of media coverage by the late 1970s. Knowledge that folk clubs were proliferating was often sufficient impetus for the formation of a nucleus of interest. I spoke to Kenny Hadden, who plays in several Scottish folk bands:

> *NLM*: How did you first get involved?
> *K*: When I was 16 at school. There wasn't any traditional music in the area that we were in touch with. There wasn't any folk club . . . so it wasn't to do with

local contacts. It was just something that happened ... The first thing was a
record. I used to listen to Radio Luxemburg and I heard 'Jig a Jig'. This wasn't
real traditional music – it was put in a rock idiom ...

It was common for musicians to come to perform in folk clubs from having
played in a session, where a group of musicians play together in an informal
setting, normally a pub. But more common, especially for singers, is for the
first performance to be in a folk club.

Different clubs have different policies with regard to floor singers. Performers have to approach the MC if they wish to perform. However, this
normally operates informally, and, unless there are a very large number of
floor performers, those who ask to be put on are put on. If a greater than
expected number of floor singers or musicians turn up on a particular night an
effort will be made to put on as many as possible, for instance by giving them
short spots of two items, or by curtailing the length of the guest spot. In many
clubs there is a book at the entrance door in which floor performers put their
names, and from which the MC will call upon floor spots. This provides an
extremely open means of access to becoming a performer. As one informant
put it: 'It's the only music you can participate in without an audition.'

In some clubs the 'book-on-the-door policy' is taken to the length that the
selection of performers is taken in strict order of entry in the book. One floor
singer at a club in Aberdeen which operated a floor singer policy such as this,
explained to me how this was her means of entry into the club.

> *E*: I went down one night and I had been a member for a few months and I
> finally summed up enough confidence, went and had a few pints in the hotel
> and said 'Right I am going to sing'. I put my name in the book, got up and
> sang. And nobody had heard me sing before.

No longer are there the song workshops and musical gate-keepers of the
1960s. Many social activities which centre on or are associated with folk clubs
involve informal music-making and there can often be an expectation to
contribute a song or a tune. This is a floor singer at Blackmore and Chelmsford
folk clubs:

> *S*: I sang out once with the Morris [dancers] and I felt it was expected of me to
> sing a song because everybody else did. So I built up my courage and I sang a
> song and then I built up my courage again and sang a song down at Chelmsford
> [folk club].
> *NLM*: Had that ever happened in your life before – being expected to sing?
> *S*: Never. That was something else.

The social scene which revolves around folk music comprises a large
element of the appeal, and this social entry facilitates entry into a subsequent
role as a performer. This is one of the leading contemporary instrumentalists
on the folk scene, Phil Cunningham, former member of Silly Wizard:

> *NLM*: Did you actually make a conscious transition from playing classical music
> to traditional music?
> *P*: No I just kind of fell into it. I just started to enjoy some of the records that I
> brought home and started to play some of it. A lot of it sounded classical –

classical arrangements of old Irish airs – but I got into the whole scene. I enjoyed the whole social side of it and when I was given the opportunity to join the band, actually getting into the crack [fun] was actually a deciding factor as much as the music.

NLM: So was the crack different to what it had been in other forms of music?

P: It certainly was from the classical music because there was no crack involved with it – it was just practising three or four hours a day and then a competition every year and the occasional performance and that was it.

This theme was repeated many times. The transition to folk music was not just musical but also social, and not just to a different social circle but to a different form of socialising, in which active musical performance and participation were integrated. As in Phil Cunningham's case, skills acquired in other musical contexts were often applied later to folk music.

It was quite common to come across musicians who had performing experience in other genres, of all types, from classical music to rock music. This was the case for roughly half of my respondents. Many performers have described 'taking refuge' in folk music from certain aspects of the other music scene that they did not like, and the following comments of a professional folk singer, Tich Frier, were quite typical of this group:

T: I started off as a choir boy when I was seven years old in St Mary's cathedral in Edinburgh, and it went on from there and I was the head boy in that choir, and then I joined a rock 'n' roll band which put an end to the soprano voice very rapidly. Things were a bit wild in the rock 'n' roll band. Some of the places we played were a bit outrageous – full of guys who wanted to realign your features. So me and the lead guitarist decided that folk music was a much safer bet – when I was about sixteen.

NLM: As simple as that?

T: Yes. There was loads of guys who were just crazy in those days. Their girlfriend would be stood at the side and would say 'I think he's lovely' and they would just go up and say 'I'll soon fix that' and jump up on the stage and whop you one. So it was a lot safer on the folk scene really.

Another common response was some familiarity or awareness of folk music outwith the context of the folk revival. This is Paul James of Blowzabella, a semi-professional English instrumental folk band:

A lot of it was to do with where I grew up, Newbury – a fairly uninteresting place to grow up. But being that bit further away from big cities there was a tiny, tiny folk music element. My best friend who I grew up with – his father . . . played guitar and had a large repertoire of folk songs as did my friend's mother.

So that got me rolling. And being interested in social history at school. And wanting to play music at school was the other reason I got involved in traditional music. This very basic sort of music appealed to me and a lot of it, compared to the stuff they wanted to teach you, is fairly undemanding technically. So I taught myself to play various woodwind instruments and it all escalated from there. I went off into rock, then folk rock, always maintaining a parallel interest in traditional music which has grown over the years.

It is possible to list several key factors which frequently interplayed in the early 'career' of a revival folk musician: first, contact with folk music, but not necessarily live contact; second, an entry into music-making through learning to play an instrument occurring outwith the folk scene; finally, performance of folk music as a means of entry into the social life of the scene.

Socialisation and the nature of the musical event

We can begin to see the acquisition of musical taste as a multi-faceted process in which differing social and musical factors interplay. Individual folk musicians have frequently had a lot of contact with other musical forms. It is important not to see the formation of musical preferences outwith the context of their relationship to other types of music, and to hold this clearly in view when trying to understand the formation of musical taste sociologically. This is the reason why I feel that this study has a wider import. The folk revival does not just affect its adherents. It also relates to and draws from non-adherents and itself influences other musical genres, even if only by acting as a negative reference point.

This articulation between genres causes a diffusion of musical ideas and also of people. People acquire new tastes as performers and audience through being active within more than one genre. This causes a diffusion of musical ideas and can lead to a rearticulation of the socio-musical aesthetic of a genre. When different models of behaviour, pertaining directly to the performing of the music and associated behaviour, cross from one genre to another there are many possible outcomes. The new form can be assimilated and made to conform to the new socio-musical aesthetic. There can be a point of conflict when an individual brings new expectations of appropriate behaviour and behaves in ways inappropriate to the aesthetic. The conflict may resolve in the resocialisation of these individuals or in some degree of normative evolution of the genre.

In this context it is important to track processes of socialisation within a genre. This is an extension of what I have termed above 'ways in', moving on from an examination of the socialisation of initiates to the ways that the normative cohesion of the folk scene as a genre is more generally restated and reaffirmed. At this point I would like to draw a few conclusions with regard to socialisation and the nature of the musical event.

While rigid boundaries cannot be drawn around given musical genres and endless subdivisions are possible, for instance to delineate various sub-genres of the folk scene, I would maintain that the central organising concept is one of cohesion of performance and audience values rather than common musical style. There is a central cohesion with regard to norms of behaviour in performance for both performers and audience. This cohesion is not 'given' but has to be affirmed and stated, restated and reaffirmed. When this cohesion of a genre is challenged from without, this reassertion, this restating of the rules can be rendered particularly apparent.

The affirmation of the central organising concepts, in however vague or non-concrete a manifestation, is closely bound to processes of socialisation. On one level socialisation adapts newcomers to the mores of the genre but it also reaffirms them for the more stalwart attenders. In the tussles that pull and push with regard to expectations of behaviour, processes of socialisation that on one level can be understood as the socialising of initiates also underscore the existence of common norms within the genre, and thus its very existence as a genre.

In looking at examples of the socialisation of performers and audiences in the folk scene, and at certain examples of pressures and rule-breaking, we discover more about the central organising concepts or ethos. To call them 'central organising concepts' is to impose my term as an analyst. But there are features which mark out the folk scene as a genre and which make it cohere. Every social occasion imposes expectations of behaviour. These derive from the expectations of those present and the extent to which the social occasion is part of a pattern of similar occasions. It does not matter whether we are talking of an orchestral concert or a bus queue. A certain normative cohesion exists, but it is possible for this to vary, as any English traveller applying English codes of queuing behaviour in France will certainly find out.

In a musical genre there are expectations of behaviour relating to the musical focus of the event which go far beyond that which could be described as 'musical'. Yet there remains a central link between the musical and this para/extra-musical behaviour. If a unified set of normative expectations in a given social domain could define a musical genre it might be worthwhile seeking to extend the terminology beyond that of artistic genres. Perhaps there is not a great deal of distinction to made in this regard between musical genres and, say, sporting ones. The cohesion of a genre creates a set of do's and don'ts, a series of expectations. A feature of many of these is that they can seem quite minor and may not be readily apparent to the uninitiated. Many of them are also commonly broken, and it is in the reactions to these that the unifying features of the genre become apparent. The following are examples of where I perceived a tension concerning a particular happening or where certain conflictual situations were pointed out to me. One concerns how folk bands wish to be appreciated; the form of response, mood or appreciation folk bands regard themselves as trying to engender in their audiences. Here are the views of members of one semi-professional Scottish folk band:

M: If you are not out there to entertain you might as well sit in the bath. Once I go out there I switch on to what I'm singing about. It's the music that switches me on. I enjoy what I am singing. So once I've started singing and I have overcome my original shyness, I am away. If get a rapport with an audience it lifts me. That's the buzz you can get; that you can surpass your normal ability. I hope that we don't bore people but I won't compromise. I won't aim to please.

I: We used to have terrible arguments with John in the group. He is probably the finest bodhran player I have ever heard. And John would always say in the middle of an instrumental I'll do a bodhran solo because that'll really get them going. And it did. They all went daft and then we both said no. That's being calculating about an audience. You're selling your music short. Playing for the reaction. That's not what we're trying to do.

This was a common comment. It is not generally considered acceptable for folk performers to be overtly calculating with an audience, to whip them up to a fervour in a deliberate way. The music is regarded as 'above' this:

> *M*: I'll sing songs that I like and they are good songs and I hope that the audience can identify with them too. It's not phony. It's what I really feel about those songs. I want them to say 'We'll really listen to this'.

> *I*: It's the easiest thing in the world to get an audience stamping their feet if that's what you are wanting. If you go up there for the reaction and [to] get people screaming . . . it is quite easy to do. You do pick your programme to go down as well as you can but I don't like groups like the Tannahill Weavers who just went out there to raise their audience to a fever pitch so that they were screaming for more at the end. People like Ossian will go up there and play their music with great conviction.

This is linked to what it is that adherents felt that the folk revival had revived. I spoke to Alistair Anderson, a solo professional folk musician:

> The basic thing . . . is that the music is what is central and is what people must go away with. The music and the contact with the musician. The music must make contact. They must not go away with the presentation. The presentation must, absolutely must be in order to get them to stay and listen to the music using stories, sometimes funny, or discussions about the instrument or quite humorous ones on the history, or on the people that I've learned things from, or what have you. Mixing light-hearted with some fairly meaty information you converse with the people which makes a contact with them. And you use that plus the balance of the programme to get them on your side so that at each point you say just enough that they are drawn in, that they want to hear the next thing and then you play the next piece. But it must always be a balance and you are never sure of the extent that you get it right.

This is an important point with relation to the folk scene's ambivalent regard to humour. Touring folk performers have told me that heckling from the audience made a good evening for them, if the humour was in no way malevolent. It served to emphasise the audience's appreciation for what they were doing. It was not a lowering of the import of what they were doing, not a desire to make the performance any less intellectual. In several instances I observed heckling and humour functioning to heighten attention. The following comments are from Derek Brimstone, a singer and one of the 'funny men' of the folk scene, and I asked him about the role of humour in his performance:

> *D*: I like to think of myself as a singer of songs and a guitarist. I don't do funny songs. People say 'do one of them funny songs'. Well, I only know about four. My songs are straight – you'll have noticed the other night. But I do rabbit on between them. But I do sing good folk songs and I do play good guitar behind them. And they say something and most of the chat is geared around telling people about the songs before I do it. You can't do that in a working men's club. You'd die on your arse.
> *NLM*: So you're saying the audiences will give you a serious listen as well?
> *D*: Oh yeah. They'll catch on. They're bright. They know what you're talking about. I've done working men's clubs and I've done things there that have sailed straight over their head. And you know you're in trouble right from the

start. They don't want to listen, they just want either background music or a bloke standing there, leaning on a mike stand with a guitar at the tips of his fingers and spouting out joke, joke, joke, joke. Well I can't do that.

These comments point to a key aspect of the nature of the folk performer–audience relationship. The humour sought in the folk scene, an important component of a 'good night', is rarely of the 'and now this is all meant to be funny' form. Rather there is a dynamic range. There is a variation in the modalities of the performance within which the humour stands out precisely for its contrasts. Derek Brimstone marks such changes abruptly in his performance, and just as humour depends on the juxtaposition of images, so this instantaneous change of mood enhances not only the humorous elements, adding a light-hearted air to the occasion, but also enhances and draws attention to the serious way that he wants his songs to be listened to. The humour heightens the intensity of the evening, at its most basic by gaining attention, and is then used to underscore the folk songs themselves, but not so as to intrude and become a focus in itself.

The humour becomes a staging device, and it is important to note in Brimstone's comparison with a working men's club that the device could not work in the same way; that his humour, if it had to stand alone as humour, would not then work. The juxtaposition of seriousness amidst wild hilarity was not a device that could be comprehended in the same way. The humour was not functioning as entertainment. It had to be understood in terms of providing a framework around the performance of his song repertoire.

The audience in a folk club does expect to be taxed to a certain extent. This was a point that Martin Carthy, one of the most important singers of the folk scene, made concerning folk audiences. It did not matter how quiet they were, he felt his performance demanded that the audience give something back. Audiences which did not he described as 'voyeuristic' and he felt that for an audience to sit passively with an air of 'now entertain me' was alien to the folk scene.

A feature of folk music in its prior context outwith the folk revival was ready performability. And this remains in the revival. Many folk festivals have a 'club room', an event which emulates a folk club and allows ordinary folk festival attenders to perform. They are generally held in small rooms, which can get very crowded. I attended one at Whitby Folk Festival where the MC had arranged a programme on the basis of those who had volunteered to perform. The room was very full, with people having to sit cross-legged on the floor in front of the front row of seats. The group who were about to come on next were obviously not used to this aspect of the folk scene. One of the group announced to the MC just before they were about to go on that 'You'll have to clear the front row to get the gear in', to which the MC brusquely replied, 'Oh no we won't'. After a pause the MC asked 'What can you do?', meaning without a lot of 'gear'. Eventually they ended up singing acoustically, squeezed against the wall, and afterwards grumbled to the MC.

What is the underlying significance of some of these social concomitants of the music, such as ready performability? Are there elements over and above the songs and tunes themselves that have also been 'revived'? And if so, why are some features taken and not others? From the above I would argue that links can be drawn, not just between the musical, that is, the sound forms, but also in the carry-over of wider aspects of 'the musical event' (Stone 1982). Certain features could be pointed to in the folk music revival. It is a music which in a sense demands to be listened to, that is to say, it cannot function as background music, and thereby creates an expectation of audience–performer communication. But it is ironic that this may have shifted the social location of the music – for the 'music of the people' to have acquired a middle-class, even academic, pretention and seriousness. It is, then, interesting to ask what is the nature of this appeal to this group in its contemporary context.

Early attempts at massification were restricted to the concert hall and the standardisation of the musical form through the filter of notation. It is not surprising that the forms of music-making of most people would not have been rigidly separated off as music, but would, more readily than today, enter people's everyday lives to form a part of social occasions, mixed with story-telling, dancing and other forms of social interaction. It was an integral element of week-to-week social interaction. This is well documented in studies of the folk tradition and it has remained so into recent times – for instance, in the case of the surviving folk singing traditions in East Suffolk documented by Dunn (1980). The intimacy of such performance settings and the nature of 'ready performability' would have prevented the emergence of stark separation between performers and audience. A crucial point is that this music evolved in and for small communities in situations where the performer and the audience actually knew each other.

Not to listen to someone singing in close proximity would have been akin to not listening to someone in direct conversation. Certain people were more talented musically, and recognised as such, but there was not an established panoply of structures separating an audience as such from performers. Thus the demands to listen were structured by the particular nature of social interaction, especially the absence of massification. Today this is no longer true. The massification of the performing arts has utterly transformed the forms of social interaction surrounding them. That is not to say that intimate music-making does not continue to exist, and the folk scene is far from being its only repository today, but it is no longer a societal norm. Intimate music-making does not occur outwith the context of more prevalent forms of musical action.

What is odd is that the folk scene should consciously seek to import such forms of audience–performer relationship. It does not appear to have occurred in the earlier folk song revival associated with Sharp. A feature of the contemporary folk revival is the search not just for the song texts and melodies of the folk tradition, but also the search for song style, in an attempt to replicate the manner in which the songs were sung. The reason for the revival of this element is very important to an understanding of the meaning of the folk revival. Certainly this search for style is perceived as a search for a degree of authenticity, in part a reaction to the arrangements of English folk song which have come down from Sharp's time which are heavily influenced by classical music. The 'second' folk revival may not just be a search for a lost or dying heritage, an attempt to salvage a distinctly English (or Scottish) ethnic music, but could also be functioning as a reaction against the massification of music.

The self-consciousness of the construction of forms of interaction is a feature which would mark it out from the folk tradition. A conscious demand to be taxed, to participate, to enter 'into' the songs, to listen to them in an intense way, is to add a certain intellectualisation, one which now pervades the folk scene. The search to revive 'the music of the people' has resulted in a movement of intellectuals and the middle class which steadfastly refuses to re-enter the domain of the genuinely popular in the numerical sense (with limited exceptions). This has much to do with many of the specific characteristics of the English folk song tradition, the nature of its demise and the nature of attempts at its revival. It is the ultimate irony that the 'music of the people' cannot be readily taken back to them. It does not fit into working men's clubs for instance, and has to remain in the refuge of the folk clubs, as if in a musical ghetto.

That the folk scene arose from certain origins under specific circumstances and has survived its initial burst of widespread popularity should not lead us to misunderstand its present manifestation. The revival is not a cultural hangover. For it to have survived is to admit of reasons for that survival. The folk scene has a sustaining organising dynamic, one which is also changing and adapting. In the next chapter I will focus on aspects of this dynamic and ask what they contribute to the normative cohesion of the genre.

7 Revival and Re-enaction

The British folk scene has deliberately and consciously established a link with the past through its attempt to revive folk song. This link is also symbolically reaffirmed by many associated features such as the venues in which many folk clubs are located. The Hoy at Anchor folk club is fairly typical in selecting the historical associations of an old pub to meet in. It has moved premises three times and each time has chosen an old pub. Certainly a feature of the folk scene is an affirmation of links with the past, through a historical feel. One comment which was typical of revival folk singers was the following from a member of a professional Scottish folk band:

> *I:* You get feelings when you play tunes that are hundreds of years old and hear songs that are hundreds of years old that are still relevant. I get this amazing feeling of being close to this whole period of history. It's a link with the past.

But is the folk revival merely an 'invented tradition' (Hobsbawm and Terence 1983) establishing continuity with a suitable historic past along similar lines to the choice of a Gothic style for the nineteenth-century reconstruction of the Houses of Parliament and much of the pageantry associated with the modern British monarchy? It might also be possible to seek an explanation more in terms of parody and kitsch than the symbolic reaffirmation of historical continuity or association. Philip Norman (1986), in an interesting article in the *Sunday Times*, pointed to the revival of old-style decoration in pubs:

> The look is uniform – a dark green, scarlet or black exterior, ornamented with flowery, fake copperplate phrases suggesting the heavy-handed plenitude of gin palaces a century ago. 'Fine Old Ales' in Keg & Bottle . . . Rare Imported Sherries & Brandies . . . Sumptuous Cold Collations Always Available.'
>   Not that customers in such places ever seriously imagine themselves back in the era of gaslight and barrel-organs, rubbing shoulders with Sherlock Holmes . . . There is a weary power of translation in us all which automatically substitutes

tepid fizz for 'Fine Old Ales', and processed ham and brow-beaten lettuce for 'Sumptuous Cold Collations'. In all these parody pubs up and down the land, one hears no murmur of protest or resentment.

For Norman this is the age of parody, of bogusing, of the celebration and the affording of a reverence to the trappings of the past but not with any attempt to reproduce any aspect of it as it was, instead replacing it with 'a parody of the past where masquerade and reality are inseparable'. If this is one way in which the past is 'used' by the present, is this also what the folk scene is doing?

One of the questionnaire respondents summed up the folk scene thus:

Some folkies stick their heads in the sand of dead culture. Some folkies see the music as embodying and reflecting change and conflict in contemporary society. Both are widespread. Most folkies embrace a bit of both.

'A bit of both' would be my own summing up of the folk scene. There are a small proportion of people who attend folk scene events and attempt to dress in a rustic manner – for instance, wearing a smock and holding a shepherd's crook. At Sidmouth Folk Festival I observed one person who went around the whole time dressed in this manner, but this was also disparaged as evidence of a 'wally' attitude. When such clothing is worn for ceremonial purposes – for example, for the performance of a Mummers' play (a form of street theatre) – it is accepted. The majority of folk scene enthusiasts wear contemporary clothing. Many of the traditionalist singers make great efforts to dress in modern styles and eschew in the manner of their presentation of 'source' material any 'olde worldiness'.

The folk scene elucidates a fascinating coexistence, on the one hand as an art form building on past links and innovating in so doing, but on the other hand also functioning to ossify, as a sort of song preservation society with close links to the past and the invented traditions of old pubs and so on, becoming itself a parody of the very features it is trying to emulate. The folk scene could be seen as counter-modernising through the celebration of live active musical participation and affirming continuity with past tradition, thereby resisting a general trend of socio-musical evolution in the west. Alternatively, it may be becoming a part of the age of parody and 'bogusing'.

But rather than try to draw a conclusion at this point, I would like to examine further the relationship between the past and the present in the contemporary folk revival. How are the symbols of the past articulated and what do they celebrate?

During the course of this study I happened to attend a 'Victorian day' which is held annually in a small Victorian spa town in the Highlands of Scotland. For this day the town 'pretends' to be Victorian. People dress in Victorian clothing and period-style stalls and entertainments are set up. It occurred to me that the association and symbolic affirmation with the past which was being celebrated here was quite different from that of the folk scene. In many respects attention to historical authenticity is deliberately eschewed by the folk scene. This Victorian day, along with the Sealed Knot, or 'authentic' performances of 'early music' can be understood as re-enaction. But is a folk club or a folk festival a 're-enaction' or an 'invented tradition', or indeed something else?

This is a difficult question to answer. There is a close parallel between the revival of folk song and its insertion into a modern context, and the revival of vernacular and traditional architectural styles in some modern buildings. For instance, one section of the British left interprets the criticisms of modernist architecture of HRH Prince Charles as an embracing of the 'kitsch of post-modernism' (Nairn 1988), while another strand interprets this as a celebration of historical continuity, reinserting nature and the human scale into a modern architectural context.

As here such interconnections are difficult to dissociate, especially given the intermingling of strands of re-enaction, nostalgia and postmodernism. The reaction against modernism has itself become a fashion, where to eschew the past in the celebration of all that is modern has now become passé. The past is now fashionable again.

The specific articulation with the past as celebrated within the folk scene might be understandable in any of the following terms: as 'fakesong'; as re-enaction; as a part of a general postmodernist trend following the decline of modernism; as parody; as kitsch. But to ascertain which is dominant requires paying close attention to how associations are articulated in a contemporary context, that is, to look at how elements of the past are articulated as symbols and to attempt to ascertain how the articulation of the form of the symbol now relates to the meaning of that symbol.

In a re-enaction the past is bounded symbolically. Attention is paid to authenticity, but the event should not be judged in modern terms. A battle re-enaction is a form of drama, not an attempt to train a civilian militia. An 'early music' recital attempts to be authentic, and part of the statement it makes is that the music is not to be judged by modern aesthetic standards. Can the folk scene be understood in terms of re-enaction? I found this a difficult question even to attempt to answer, for there seemed to be no clear method as to how to answer it. But in carrying out this study certain clues presented themselves.

While at Sidmouth Folk Festival I was watching a Morris dance 'side', the term used to describe a team of dancers. There was much fooling around associated with the dancing and a large crowd had gathered. Morris sides normally have a 'fool' whose job is to ritualise the tomfoolery and add an appearance of chaos to the dancing – weaving in and out, hitting dancers with an inflated bladder and so on. While watching these antics one feature struck me in particular: the fool's 'bladder' was not a bladder but an inflated rubber kitchen glove.

The imagery of the fool derives from the past. The fool of 'traditional' Morris sides is an institution which has carried over into the folk revival. Most modern Morris sides have a fool. But in this instance while a tradition has been 'revived', there was also an element of debunking. This is very different from 'old' music re-created for 'early music' recitals. The use of the rubber glove was a 'send-up' of those who pay close attention to authenticity. But I would argue that that 'sending up' could indicate a deeper symbolic function. Re-enaction suspends the present. A re-enacted event of any sort is not to be judged by the aesthetic criteria and artistic values of today; judgement pertaining to these criteria is suspended. Appreciation derives from the authenticity of re-enaction. However, this Morris side was demonstrating a very different view of its activities and the rubber glove could be a key to understanding this. The rubber glove was an ostentatious and deliberate intrusion of the present. Its presence was made manifest in humour, but the import of its intrusion was none the less significant for that. The glove actually affirms, not suppresses, the fact that the organising concept here is not 're-enaction', but 'revival'.

There is a fundamental difference between re-enaction and revival, and each represents a different structuring ethos. Re-enaction implies a suspension of the present, allowing the past to be entered into, but in a bounded sense. Revival also requires that the past be 'entered' in some symbolic way, but once so entered artistic integrity is not so threatened by the intrusion of the present. It is entered 'once again' but allows continuity through a process of artistic evolution. Composition within a revived genre is permitted and encouraged.

For a re-enaction, the intrusion of the present would shatter the authentic integrity of the artistic event which therefore has to be shielded from such intrusion – to be 'boxed' or 'framed' (Goffman 1974). This framing also fits the performance ethos, itself a conscious framing necessitated by the staging inherent in most of the performing arts. But for this Morris side at Sidmouth Folk Festival their performance was frequently and deliberately disrupted; the performance itself was suspended. The Morris side was dancing in a pub back yard, so small that while dancing, access to the bar was blocked. There were adults and children, even the odd dog milling around, with people barging past the dancers as they danced. The event was not programmed. It was not staged. It was one of the 'here-and-now' events that is characteristic of the folk scene. The audience had not come to view this performance but had happened upon it by chance. By dancing in such a context the dancers were themselves making a powerful artistic statement to revive an art form and place it in the present. The rubber glove symbolises and accentuates this intrusion. Many Morris sides now create their own dances, some within the style of existing 'traditions', and even consciously create new dance traditions. This points to a similar conclusion of re-entry rather than re-enaction. The same is true of folk song. The majority of folk singers, including those most wedded to the folk traditions and 'source' material, quite readily sing recently composed material.

But could this event be summed up as parody? This would be inadequate as an explanatory concept because parody implies a suppression of humour, and the suppression of attention to, and questioning of, the very inauthenticity which is its characteristic.

The use of the glove and the bladder has important symbolic connotations. From observations of other Morris sides in performance I noticed that some did use real bladders, and these sides tended to 'send up' the music to a far lesser degree. The fool fooled less and such sides took the music more seriously, following dance traditions to the letter and dancing in staged circumstances, for instance at organised 'Morris Ring' meets of dance sides.

Thus I am suggesting what may seem a paradoxical symbolic interpretation of the bladder and the glove. Historically the bladder would have been used because it was at hand. It was the most readily available object that was suitable. The latex glove comes closer to symbolising this being 'at hand' than the use of a pig's bladder today which is contrived and points to 'olde worldiness' and re-enaction. To venerate it in this way as an authentic reconstruction is to place a symbolic value upon it which I doubt it ever had in the folk tradition. To place this degree of seriousness upon the authenticity of the reconstruction of the form of the dance is to change its function and use in performance.

Morris dancing and its East Anglian equivalent, Molly dancing, always was an excuse for a beer, a dance, a song, a chance to get out of the house and so on – see, for instance, Humphries (1985). The fact that these were functions that Morris dance served in the folk tradition should make us look away from an over-concentration upon forms to their use, function and meaning. In this context the use of a latex rubber glove may place this particular Morris side closer to the folk tradition, in terms of reviving certain essential symbolic and functional meanings, than does an 'authentic' reconstruction through the use of a pig's bladder. Morris dance was and is a 'low' art form, to be contrasted with the state dance troupes and the ritualised ballet-cum-drama infusions that have characterised much folk dance revival throughout Europe. The framing of dance into spectacle is closely bound with re-enactment.

Re-entry contradicts this and places an immediacy upon the event. Exactly the same applies to Mummers' plays, a form of street theatre which the folk revival has also revived from the folk tradition and which is often performed at folk festivals. It is no coincidence that the folk revival has borrowed these forms directly from the British folk traditions and set about placing them in similar contexts together; reviving their forms as formulae for re-creation rather than in terms of formulaic re-enactment.

While there may be an air of chaos surrounding the Morris in terms of the antics of the fool and the staging of the event, the dances are taken seriously. There is no interference with repertoire. In contrast, many state dance teams draw from their native folk traditions but take a vernacular value and 'elevate' it. The rubber glove, in contrast, symbolises the intrusion of a contemporary vernacular value, accentuating the status of the dance form as 'low' art and thereby preventing status elevation. The glove may thus be functioning as a very potent symbol. The very ambivalence of the symbol enhances this aspect of it. It could be read as a straight 'send-up', it also accentuates the here-and-now, but it also symbolises the modern and forcibly intrudes an artefact of the present into the performance and in so doing destroys allusions which hark back to a 'lost England'. At Sidmouth Folk Festival there were many features which led to similar conclusions. For instance, in the festival newsletter I noted that there was even a workshop for 'creating a new tradition'.

Interpreting symbols is difficult and it is easy for the investigator's imagination to take over, especially since so much of the symbolic is not overtly stated. It is difficult to forward a null hypothesis for symbolic significance. I was therefore interested to come across a couple of articles in *The Morris Dancer* which articulated some thoughts by Morris dancers on the nature of tradition and revival in Morris dancing. Morris dancing is widely regarded as epitomally English. In Aberdeenshire, Scotland, there is a Morris side which performs dances mainly from the Cotswold traditions of England and which was the subject of a debate in this magazine. An article by Bill Banbury (1981) presented evidence that Morris dancing had been performed in Scotland and under this name. In Perth museum there is even a dancer's costume. The article argued that since Morris had been danced in Scotland, Scottish Morris sides should seek to incorporate those features of the Scottish Morris dance as could be ascertained from historical reference. Banbury suggested that the Cotswold titles of the dance team (bagman, squire, etc.) could be replaced by more appropriate Scottish or local titles – laird, or in Aberdeenshire, Abbott or Prior of Bonaccord – and that it would be more appropriate to celebrate Scottish than English festivals. He also suggested a reconstruction of the Perth Glovers' dance based upon surviving contemporary descriptions of its dance and costume. He suggested that Scottish tunes of the sixteenth and seventeenth centuries which were known to have had a wide currency, and are preserved in Court music collections, could be used.

I think it is worth quoting the reply of Don French (1982), foreman of Banchory Morris men, at some length:

> The old Scottish traditions – yes, we are very much aware of them – probably more so than most Scots. Most of the references quoted by [Banbury] were already known to us, though there were a few new details. But there is, I think a great danger in such matters of confusing 'traditional' with 'antiquarian'. For example, we use some of the old holidays, like May, Beltane, and, being near Aberdeen, Bon-Accord, as the Morris seems to fit naturally into present-day festivities on these occasions. On the other hand the modern Scottish 'Yule', at least around Deeside, just doesn't exist in the old way, so, while we do dance in the Christmas/New Year period generally, there is no one time or place at which we dance, as there is at the other times.
>
> The suggestion of using Scottish terms for dignitaries is likewise maybe a bit forced. Anyway, we can't use Abbott and Prior of Bonaccord, as they still exist in Aberdeen. Also many of the titles are more generalised 'Lords of the Feast' than specific to the Morris. A generic term like 'Laird' for 'Squire' might serve, but it's still pretty contrived . . . 'Bagman' is every bit as good north of the Border as south.
>
> Similarly, with music, I must confess ignorance of most 16th/17th century court music, but, in principle, don't see why it has any better claim to be used for Morris tunes than, say, 'Bonny Banchory', 'The Hen's March to the Midden', or 'Charlie is m'Darlin'' – all of which, as well as a couple of original tunes in similar idiom, we use for our own dances.
>
> That's right – our own dances. For we have, in Banchory, the beginnings of a new 'tradition'. Some is adapted from the Cotswold style. Other parts are quite different. But all is an attempt to work towards something that feels right when done in this area. A gradual, trial-and-error build-up of this kind may, in the long

run, achieve a more truly traditional whole than trying to resurrect exactly what went on in pre-Reformation Scotland, which itself no longer exists and is, in that sense, every bit as alien as any 'English' import. Give us another three or four hundred years. If we're still going by then, it should have all been licked into shape sufficiently for some latter-day Cecil Sharp to come and 'collect' it.

Thus, though we had a look at what we could learn of the Perth Glovers' dance – for it does look tantalisingly worth having a go at it – in the end we have not tried to 're-construct' it, as there is so little detailed description that the amount of imagination necessary to fill in the gaps would require rather the invention of a completely new dance. So – bearing in mind the Scottish Sword Traditions, the hints of Rapper style in the Perth dance, all the background information available to us, and the old local custom of the deer drive . . . we did just that. The result is the Banchory Ternan Horn Dance. This is a sword dance for five men, plus a sixth man dressed in a deerskin and carrying a pair of antlers, who ends up being 'beheaded' when the final lock/nut/what-you-will is woven around the antlers so as to hold them when exhibited at the end of the dance.

We can see here the invention of a new tradition, but it would be dangerous to read too much into the notion of 'invented tradition' or to introduce an overly pejorative characterisation of this process. Within a revival an attempt can be made to return to similar aspects of symbolic function of the 'source' social context, as with the intrusion of the rubber glove already described.

The folk scene has moved on from being a conscious attempt to re-create, preserve and rearticulate Britain's vernacular musical heritage, towards being a genre whose central function is to celebrate live, accessible, small-scale music-making. The historical development of the folk scene is no longer locked in the 'taxidermist' approach to traditional music. In fact, by having secured a crucial link with the past – by refocusing attention on social history outwith the confines of the school history syllabus, and having to a certain extent achieved this, the importance of collected 'source' material is now declining in the folk scene. Historical continuity has also come to be celebrated in another way, not by slavishly copying traditional songs, but by composing modern songs about historical themes.

The folk scene is now a genre whose central dynamic is no longer the reliving of the past, but affirming a certain articulation with it. In the early folk revival the articulation with the past was fought out as an ideological struggle but this fervour has now largely departed. By taking traditional songs almost for granted for the very reason that they now do not need preserving or reviving, the folk scene is looking forwards. The songs in performance are changing in function and, ironically, may be now more closely mirroring their original function than they did earlier in the folk revival.

British folk music is unusual among revivals of traditional music in seeking to place past 'low' culture at its core, not seeking to elevate it to 'high' culture as in the mode of many eighteenth- and nineteenth-century European composers, the 'first' English folk revival, and in the form taken by the interest of the Victorians in Scottish traditional music. Instead, the aim is to maintain accessibility to the music, to allow the form to superimpose itself on new songs composed in the genre and extend the stylistic form itself. But artistic accessibility remains at the core – the fact that the music can be performed by anyone and not only by highly trained individuals. Conviviality and accessibility remain centre-stage.

This may be the key ethnomusicological link. It is why traditional 'source' singers have been welcomed into the folk scene, but also why new songs can be composed and performed on the same stage by revival singers and musicians. The musical elements in traditional song have been carefully re-worked but they remain embedded because they still contain many of the same values. The music has not been transposed by the folk scene to the drawing room or to an orchestral setting, although the music has changed. For instance, the use of new technology and the rise of professionalism have transmuted the meaning of the music and the musical event in the folk scene. This will be discussed in greater depth later.

However, it is my argument here that historical continuity functions as a vehicle for transmitting potent associated symbolism such as the celebration of participation and accessibility. Historical continuity has a central role not just for reasons of a nostalgic articulation with a past that people are sorry to see disappear but because history does itself demonstrate continuity, and its celebration in music ensures that the musical 'artefacts' themselves have a greater role and significance than the individuals who happen to be carrying and transmitting them at any one point in time. A culture or art form having few if any links with its past enhances and accentuates the present. An art form with a strong sense of its past depresses the attention to self and the cult of individualism.

An issue to raise here is the articulation of the concept of revival with that of genre. Whereas the music of the British folk traditions was the music of specific localities, the music created by the folk scene has become a genre whose boundaries are not locally specific. The folk revival has created a genre and is also one of the points of Harker's (1985) criticism. In many ways the revival of a pre-existing musical form in the confines of a genre entails the pre-selection of that which is to be revived. Thus Harker points to the selectivity of much of Sharp's song-collecting. I believe that such an opinion focuses too much upon the song as an artefact rather than musical performance.

In the British folk tradition musical performance was tightly bound by locality. It was a vernacular music, 'performed', moulded and shaped in the general course of people's daily life. A musical form which has at its centre the encouragement of people to sing and play while minimising the hierarchical tendencies in the production of music as commodity may in fact be the key element which has been 'revived'. The songs can be seen as artefacts and it might be that their importance may not be their revival as artefacts, a notion which derives from an over-concentration upon form and product. Rather than questioning the validity of attempts to reinsert past traditions into con-temporary settings, perhaps what should be questioned is the oddity of cul-tural forms which seek their 'roots' externally or which even seek to accentuate and celebrate their discontinuity, their divorce from indigenous cultural roots.

Elsewhere in the world traditional and modern popular musics are nothing like so separated from each other as in Britain. In Britain the separation of youth culture from its cultural heritage separates history from the present. Traditional music and culture serve as a repository not just of historical 'facts' but of collective experience. Just as the function of the traditional arts was to serve as a repository of experience and also of knowledge, the separation of these functions in the modern world is a very recent product of consumer culture. Music as an element of the vernacular, something that people do, has become a commodity – something they buy and can no longer do. The folk scene may be a reaction to this, and the form of its articulation with the past a powerful symbolic means of resisting commodification. We may be seeing the intertwining of the medium and the message; neither communicates symbolically without the other. The text and the form of its transmission together create the message. The insertion of certain vernacular values into the modern British folk revival is as important as the content of the song texts and melodies. It is the mode of their production that we should look at and is the reason why I have deliberately moved away from a concentration on textual analysis which bedevils so much literary and musical analysis.

The association with the past, and a particular past at that, the culture of ordinary people, is the assertion of a certain set of values in artistic production. It is also a celebration of a certain mode of artistic production. It is here that the greatest divergence between the 'high' arts and the 'low' arts is to be found – the arts which are the statements of working-class people cannot be wrapped up in the manner of artistic forms transmitted through pedagogy, or which celebrate hierarchy and centralised control – they cannot be 'put in evening dress' and still carry the same meaning. This is, in essence, why the music of the high and low arts cannot be judged by the same aesthetic and artistic criteria.

The role of the past in the music might be interpreted as the celebration of a rediscovered celebration of ethnicity, but it is the celebration of an ethnicity tied to a specific ideology. The content and forms of the cultural production of the genre serve to reassociate the adherents with a certain set of values. It is not the realisation of Sharp's 'national music'.

It may be no coincidence that the folk scene has attracted a disproportionately large number of the upwardly mobile middle class in the service sector, as indicated by the folk club audience survey. These people are one generation removed from working-class origins, from the memory of social hardship and collective social solidarity. Yet these people in their new social location find little to identify with in terms of elite culture and resist the cultural passivity of middle-class Britain. In suburban Britain music does not function as a medium of community expression; it does not serve to express 'individuality in community' (Blacking 1973).

An affirmation of a link with the past can function as a complicated ideological statement and in music, as in architecture, more interesting than assertions of parody, pastiche, or kitsch (which are mere assertions of 'false consciousness' in a fancy wrapping), is the issue of how the features of the past are manipulated as symbols. Do they carry a new symbolic load – for example, 'bogusing' – or can a certain symbolic function be maintained – for example, 're-entry'?

The British folk scene certainly exudes an odd contradiction. On the one hand it exists as a reaction to a dominant culture based on parody and nostalgia which has torn culture from the vernacular, from its function of embedding the identity of people into their socio-historical context. On the other hand it has become part of that culture. It is itself a constituent element of the age of parody which heralds the triumph of the reign of commodities over consumers. The folk clubs and festivals may be seen as small bastions of vernacular values in the creation of culture, but might they also be viewed as musical theme parks? Both models can be seen articulated in the folk scene. The folk scene incorporates elements of re-enaction and re-entry. To ascertain which is dominant will require further resolution in an examination of the mode of cultural production. The folk scene is indeed mediated by the cash nexus, but in a very specific form. Who is buying? Who is selling? Who is gaining? Who is expropriating? What is the relationship between the 'impresarios' and the musicians, between the audiences and the performers, between those who are paid for their services and those who consume those services?

8   *Success and the Professional Folk Performer*

The way in which the folk scene relates to financial matters has moulded the form of evolution of musical performance in the folk scene in highly specific ways. The folk scene as a whole, in terms of the organisation and management of its events, the promotion of artists, its handling of publicity, its dealings with and profile in the mass media, is quite unlike other musical genres.

As the early folk clubs formed and started to meet regularly there were few opportunities to book guests. There were living 'source' performers, but of these, few were in touch with the folk scene. A folk club as such was something alien to these 'tradition' bearers. Thus it was the early revival performers themselves who largely came to be the first generation of visiting guest performers. This began as more popular performers came to be invited to perform at neighbouring clubs and were offered a small fee for their services. In the early days of most folk clubs such nights were infrequent. But while some performers on the folk scene may berate unprofessionalism and the existence of floor spots, another view is still often heard. No one actively recruited or promoted the first generation of touring folk club guests. In the words of one professional folk singer:

> The folk scene started with people getting together, amateurs getting together to sing and then they would have a guest and it became worthwhile for people to do that semi-professionally until there was a pro circuit, and the argument for that was that it keeps the standards up. But having spawned that system I think it does look a bit askance at people going round making their living at it.

But the possibility that a living could be made in this way prompted some of these guests to have a go. Tony Rose was one of this first generation of folk professionals. He explains how the rise of the folk professional happened almost by accident:

> This was a weird situation to find yourself in anyway. . . . There's a difference in attitude from when I went professional to today . . . Nowadays people make a

conscious decision: 'I will be a professional singer'. The only reason we did it was that most of us began singing for fun and you began to be asked to sing in other places, and one day you realise that you are singing four or five nights a week and it became then a feasible possibility to do that as a full-time living.

Today the weekly guest is the typical format for a folk club. The rise in demand for guests has been such that by 1987, according to the estimate of the director of the English Folk Dance and Song Society, there were 300 professional singers and musicians primarily dependent upon folk music for their living. The folk scene therefore contains a large contradiction: a scene that has as its central organising ethos that ordinary people can make music independent of commercialisation has spawned a generation of professionals. Most folk events involve the exchange of money.

However, the relationship between these professionals and the audiences has remained particular. To see this it would be worth obtaining a rough idea of the economics of being a folk scene performer. This was the hardest information to glean from my respondents. However, some respondents were prepared to divulge their earnings, and some other indications can be gained from the clubs themselves.

The earning potential of folk performers, even at the top end of the scene, is quite limited. For instance, one informant, a professional performer at the very top end of fee levels for a touring soloist, mentioned that while he aimed for a fee of £200 this could easily 'slip' when he was putting a tour together and that he would fill in a vacant night on a tour for as little as £90 for a 'genuine' folk club. He gives an idea of what this fee has to cover:

> If you want to do a reasonable amount of research and rehearsal, if you want to maintain a professional level of publicity and admin back-up, and a reasonably new car – and . . . as a professional I do not think that it is a professional attitude to run a car that is much more than three years old – then basically you can divide a fee by four. The expenses will halve it, and you should be spending about half your time rehearsing, doing the admin. – so you can say that the daily rate instead of being £110 is £27. Now in fact most people in this country work 225 days a year . . .
> £110 would not maintain me as a professional at the national average wage, so the higher-paid gigs abroad and the better-paid arts gigs subsidise the folk clubs. One could make a living in the folk clubs at £110 and less, and a lot . . . do, but you would have much less money to spend on maintaining a profile – you would probably be in the old banger and you would be out on the road a lot more. That's the way I started out.

The folk clubs are the backbone of the folk scene, though higher fees charged at some festivals can provide a better level of living for some. Indeed, some of the higher-earning bands have decided to drop the folk clubs altogether in favour of higher fees at folk festivals, and have also broken into, in a limited way, the arts centre circuit. A few, such as Battlefield and The Boys of the Lough, have moved out into town-centre concert circuit, but, most of those folk bands who have eschewed the folk scene altogether have then had to move away from Britain to find work throughout the year. Some, like Silly Wizard, have found that the large appeal of British folk music abroad and its less restrictive structural organisation, was such as to allow them to attain higher levels of earning if they stopped touring in Britain altogether.

Some top folk performers supplement their income by doing media work. The MacCalmans, for instance, are a top-level three-piece band who have had their own exclusive six-week TV show devoted to their own music. As a band they have attempted to remain as performers within the folk clubs and festivals, despite their popularity in performing to larger concert venues. But because the MacCalmans do also perform outwith the folk scene, Ian MacCalman explains that this has caused problems for them within it:

> *I*: After our television series, and we were one of the first Scottish bands to get an album and from those days no matter what sort of stuff we sang or where we sang it – in *Melody Maker* they classed us . . . always with groups like the Corries and the Spinners. For a fact we weren't earning the sort of money that the Corries and the Spinners were earning. We were singing three-part harmony, stuff that no one had heard. We were singing in clubs and yet somehow the myth came about that we were not only unapproachable, but almost undesirable for club gigs, and we've been putting out literature and going about the clubs saying we are still wanting to do clubs on a basis where the club cannot lose – taking a percentage of the gate. And you still get 'Oh the MacCalmans – are we going to sell out?'

Such stories were by no means uncommon. It appears that media success is taken by many within the folk scene as a sign that a group has stepped outside the folk scene. I had originally assumed that a certain stigma attaching to folk music was largely to account for its low media profile. However, it appears that there is a reluctance to embrace media success within the scene. Could it be that it is not just the case that the folk scene is under-represented in the media for reasons external to the scene, but because the folk scene itself consciously eschews media success? It certainly appears that those who do gain a certain degree of media penetration within the folk scene are given a hard time, and this is deliberate.

The most important factor with regard to the management of success and professionalism is the structure of the scene itself. The folk clubs are universally run by amateurs. There are no folk club impresarios. The events are not structured for profit. Very few folk festivals are sufficiently large to require the services of a paid director.

Folk festivals integrate informal music-making at a large number of events, which itself places restrictions of scale. Even at the largest festivals such as Sidmouth, the phenomenon of spectacle is reserved for dance display. Folk song events at festivals largely occur at the scale of audiences of under a hundred, though often with the odd 'special' main concert a little larger than this. Within most folk festivals there will be a large number of small events run on the lines of a folk club. The insertion of floor singers at these events is common.

The demands of participation place boundaries of scale upon the folk scene. This is the single most limiting factor with regard to the upper limits of the fee structure. Entrance fees have remained low, with most clubs charging between £1.00 and £2.00. The folk scene, then, has placed limitations of scale upon its performers. The lack of large-scale media penetration and record sales forces performers to draw most of their earnings from live performance. In consequence, the limitations of scale of the folk clubs force a certain uniformity upon fee levels. It is remarkable that the fees of the most respected and best-known folk touring singers are little more than three times the fee level of the most junior and novice touring singers.

But if those at the top of the scene did try to raise their fees further, they would merely put themselves out of work, because it is the structure of the events themselves which places an upper limit on the fees that can be charged. Since these are folk clubs, as opposed to weekly concerts, premises are usually selected that cannot accommodate more than a hundred people, and for a very large number of clubs it is well below this. The fee structure of the clubs remains fairly consistent on a week-to-week basis. Some clubs put up their prices on special nights, but this will only be by an amount normally less than £1.

The structure of the scene works against stardom. There are stars, but their success has to be measured in terms other than financial success, or else they have to leave and work outside the folk scene. But this affects not only the pocket of folk 'stars' but also their relationship to audiences. It prevents folk musicians aping the role models of other genres. Folk singers have to ask themselves, as Alistair Anderson put it:

> Whether they decide to look like, to try and ape the presentations of pop music, or whether they say our strengths lie elsewhere.

The folk scene does not have the same hierarchy based on monetary success, and because of that the status markers have to be articulated in other ways. The lack of stardom defined by monetary success and a certain disdain on the part of folk audiences for wider success cause the status markers identifying those at the top to work in a much more subtle fashion. Although there are status markers differentiating performers which serve to keep successful folk musicians at the 'top', it does not propel them into a different order of earnings. Status differentiation works in a very different way. Folk musicians come to feel much more ambivalent about their status since earnings are not a guide to their position, and in fact high earnings can lead to the opposite – a lowering of reputation on the folk scene itself. The definition of success cannot be that gold at the end of the rainbow.

But there is also a reverse side to the coin. With the promise of 'gold' in other genres, from rock to classical music, many musicians will put up with a lot of hardship for the prospect of possibly 'making it'. But in the folk scene even this has to be articulated differently. Once an individual is earning, he or she tends to accrue a 'going rate'. Admittedly this may be lower than for established performers, but low differentiation between the bottom and the top of the genre suggests a very different conceptualisation of the 'success trajectory' of performers on the folk scene. Ged Foley of the House Band, a professional folk band, explains:

> It is all tied down with a different time scale. It appears to be that in the mainstream if you form a band and you haven't got the record contract or the publicity or got yourself noticed within a year really you have blown it. But in the acoustic folk world it works on a longer time scale. A band can exist for a longer time and is expected to pay its dues for a longer time almost. The other thing is that I get the feeling that a lot of bands' idea of success in the folk world is to have reached a point where you are like a snowball, just doing constant work. Once you have reached that state you are not continually looking for this main chance. Realistically that's as much as you can expect. You're not being true to yourself if you think that you can have that elusive freak hit single.

The long time scale of success was a feature I noted when leafing through old folk magazines and looking at the 'what's on' lists. Many people have been touring on the folk scene for decades. There is a low turnover of performers. Most of those at the very top of the scene, such as Martin Carthy and Vin Garbutt, were also at the top ten years ago, and many of them twenty and thirty years ago, and a common complaint on the part of folk club organisers is the lack of new talent each year available to be booked in their clubs.

But a well-established reputation did not necessarily lead to a higher status; in the words of Tich Frier:

> You had this awful pang of collective consciousness which has affected the folk scene for so long. You had the whole anomalous situation, a whole series of irreconcilable situations. Professional singers came about almost by accident, and yet you had people theorising that you shouldn't have such things as a professional folk singer – a contradiction in terms. And yet they were there, whether you liked it or not. At the same time there was no professional organisation behind them and there never has been.
>
> You have a series of professionals dependent on a series of enthusiastic amateurs for their living – for the organisation in which they work, and that was always a potentially precarious situation.

The normal routes to artist–audience separation are not available to the folk singer: the audiences run the clubs; organisers provide accommodation for artists in their own homes; there is the absence of a stage door. All these features have restructured the relationship of the artist to the audience. In the folk scene, the direct participation of the audience in making music at the very same events as guests also sets up a pressure. Touring professionals are directly exposed to challenges to their status at events. Of course, it would be ridiculous to claim that to any great degree this is how a guest will view a floor singer's performance. But my argument is that the non-professional performance is an essential element within the structure of the event itself. I spoke to a floor performer at an Aberdeen folk club:

> *E*: When anyone starts to make a name for themselves they start to get cocky, but it is a phase that most people get out of, and they realise later on that 'I am a small fish in a very big sea'. Most of the artists who are 'folk stars' are not like that. People who can go on sell-out tours in the States, they will still come and

sing in a wee folk club in Aberdeen because that is their bread and butter and they know it, and they have a friendly attitude. I don't think I have ever come across anyone who has come to the club to perform that hasn't been a genuinely nice person, who to a certain extent isn't grateful for the opportunity to survive doing what they want to do.

The lack of stardom in the British folk scene makes itself felt in many ways, one of which is the general treatment of performers by audiences. On the one hand, this is usually friendly and intimate, but on the other hand touring folk performers do not enjoy the same trappings of special treatment deriving from the 'star syndrome', which accrues to touring musicians in other genres. The House Band also tours abroad; Ged Foley explains the difference with regard to touring in Britain:

> *G*: The background side of things is normally better organised. A lot more thought seems to have gone into it over there [the USA] and in Europe. I'm not knocking people over here, it's just a different way of doing things. For instance, if you turn up at a British folk club in the afternoon you can't get in because it's locked. It opens on pub hours. So that's one thing, whereas in Holland, you can arrive at 2.00 in the afternoon and there will be somebody there waiting for you. So you can set up your equipment in the afternoon. As soon as you arrive at one of these places somebody makes you a cup of coffee and offers you a sandwich. That doesn't happen here. The accommodation quite often is hotels. They'll have their own sound system, decent lighting which makes a big difference. They'll have their own advertising system. Whereas over here, it tends to be a pub and there's no lighting and no sound system and there's nobody there until about 7.00, and this sort of thing gets a bit depressing after a while.

The tensions generated by the downplaying of staging within the folk scene frustrate many performers. I spoke to Alan Taylor, a professional singer-songwriter:

> *A*: Playing to twenty people in an acoustic club is more difficult than playing to five thousand people in a concert, because it's the closeness of them, because after all you are performing. Regardless of what most folk singers might say, that 'you just sing a song', you are performing. You are standing and you are isolated, and everyone is looking at you. If you are not a performer there is no point in doing it. There is no point in just relating the song. You have got to perform the song to get something out of it. You are performing whether you like it or not. And when you are performing that close to people, it is very very difficult, because they are almost on top of you. You need this certain space between you and the audience, to assume the stage persona to perform. But when they are sitting right next to you they see you are just one of them. You are just one of them, but you also have to be something different before their very eyes.
>
> *NLM*: Is it a conflict of two roles?
>
> *A*: Yes.
>
> *NLM*: When you are in a big setting it's very clear what role you're in?
>
> *A*: Yes – it's very clear right from the start that you are the performer.
>
> *NLM*: But that other facet is the appeal of the folk scene?
>
> *A*: I think there is a certain amount of self-conning going on there. It's like dressing down. Performers and audiences will dress down to go to a folk

club. . . . That's fair enough, but there is a certain amount of dressing down, metaphorically speaking, by sophisticated middle-class people dressing down to be one of the lads . . . I find this totally insipid . . . I feel patronised and insulted by these people if I am in the audience and I don't believe them . . . If you are going to get up on stage at all you might as well accept the fact that you are going to have to be a performer. And so you have got to go for it. There's no point in saying 'Well you know I'm just like you, I'm no better no worse than you.' Well that's true and you can say I'm just learning my trade just like you. That is also true but what is not true is they've paid £2.00 to come and see you, so unless you are going to make it a singaround, a free-for-all, then you are in an artificial situation straight away.

However, forms of presentation in the folk scene are changing, as is apparent from changes which have occurred at the major English folk festival held at Sidmouth. A former director of the English Folk Dance and Society commented:

J: Sidmouth is a very interesting example because it has been going on for 32 years. Last year for the first time it lost money. The overheads are getting higher and higher. A simple thing – thirty, twenty years ago the performers were young. They would be happy to camp. Now the festival pays low fees but it provides accommodation. The cost in a seaside town in the height of the season is phenomenal and it's all those things. Twenty years ago your PA rig would be very simple indeed. Now you need a very complicated PA rig, firstly because the performers are more sophisticated and expect it. Secondly, the audience expect it. The PA rig in the arena is costing a fortune. Look at the lighting rig there. You used to be able to get away with four spotlights. The audience has got more sophisticated and expect it. You can't charge a lot more to the audience.

I did note that here in the midst of all this it was the song events that were held in the most dingy surroundings: inadequate seating and sanitation in a small cramped and unsuitable night club, for instance. The song side of the festival was almost 'hanging on' in resisting the change to slicker presentation that was occurring elsewhere in the festival, especially with regard to the presentation of the dance events. However, it must be stressed that Sidmouth is in the forefront of moves towards slicker presentation at (some of) its events. The following comment from Tony Wilson, a semi-professional folk singer, gives a more typical idea of the feel of a folk festival:

Folk festivals can be a bit of a mixed blessing. Dragging people into what seems to be the boggiest field in the county and drinking out of plastic pints in wet and unpleasant conditions seems to be slightly masochistic. It depends on the festival. Some festivals have a warm atmosphere that seems to pervade everything, everybody seems willing to join in and other places you are banging your head against a brick wall.

For a professional folk musician, the concept of success has to be understood within the overall context of the performance setting, which imposes constraints on the style of presentation. For this reason I will move on from the consideration of success specifically to a more general consideration of staging within the genre.

9 Staging and Informality

Our club audience sing like angels. We are frequently congratulated by guests on the quality and strength of our chorus singing. But ... it's not only our choruses that impress visitors ... Nearly all the best traditional music-makers study their subject and are a mine of information about the origins of tunes and lyrics. There is more enjoyment to be had if you understand a little of the background of the music and our club is famed for the rapt attention given to any explanation the performer is able to offer ... And please forgive the glares of the more seasoned members if you raise your voice between songs. Join them in giving the singer a hearing and you'll soon be able to glare as well as anyone.

(Hoy at Anchor Folk Club Newsletter, August 1973)

Attentiveness is expected of folk club audiences and tugs at the essence of informal presentation. I asked a long-standing Aberdeen folk club floor singer about the settings she preferred:

> P: I much prefer the very informal surroundings, non-orchestrated. Places like the Frigate [a pub singaround] where you can just sit down and play what you want to – where there's no demands on you. At the folk club you put your name down in the book – it's a discipline. You set yourself up and sometimes I find this audience–performer structure a little bit strange. When I'm up there I've all sorts of things going through my mind. Why are they there sitting listening to me? On the other hand what the hell am I doing here singing to these people? It's a strange human activity where you've got participants and non-participants, and it can be very unnerving while you're up there playing. But it's different when I'm playing in a very informal setting when we're all going round singing just for sheer entertainment.

The folk scene presents a series of contradictions with regard to the way it presents its musical performances: attention to explanations of songs, glaring at interruptions, a general expectation of silence during songs, heckling, going to the bar during the performance, the freedom of movement, the audience as a whole participating musically in the performance, the tolerance of a certain low level of background hubbub (mostly between songs, rarely during them), the lack of comfortable surroundings. Yet to me there seemed to be an ambivalence about the meaning and significance of many of these features. For instance, the feeling of relaxedness and informality was such that it would be possible for the uninitiated easily to confuse some folk club nights with a pub gig, and yet they are in fact quite different. On other occasions a folk club can seem like a formal concert in an inappropriate venue, though again I would take this as an unsatisfactory explanation of the performance setting for the following reason.

At relaxed musical occasions such as a pub gig, there is not the same onus to sit passively and listen as at a concert. Quite often people at folk clubs do set up conversations during the evening but these are normally people who are not familiar with the ways of behaving in the folk scene. Hence the 'glares' mentioned above. Calls of 'shhh' are fairly common at folk club events and, perhaps surprisingly, they often arouse quite a lot of ire in those to whom they are directed.

On one occasion I took along to a club someone who was not familiar with the folk scene. He proceeded to talk during the performance, fairly loudly and persistently. He was eventually asked to desist and took umbrage with the comment 'I'd come here to enjoy myself'. It became clear that quietness and direct attention to the performance was something my friend expected of a concert situation and no other. The folk club appeared very relaxed, with ready movement to the bar, people heckling, joining in the singing and even some quiet murmuring between songs. To him this was evidence of a quite different musical occasion, a pub gig where the music is in the background, to be listened to if one felt like it. This links in with the pervasiveness of the recording consciousness. Most music that is heard in our society is not heard by people as live performance. People have become accustomed through habituation to not listening to people, to not considering music as direct interpersonal communication akin to other forms of communication, especially that of speech.

Where musical listening in our society is 'demanded' it is normally segregated off, tightly partitioned into special arenas designed for this purpose – concerts. Furthermore, the presence of recording technology at live music events reinforces a mental configuration deriving from recorded music itself. It is now possible to talk over live music and for that music not to be disrupted, for the talk not to prevent or interrupt the performance. Musical performance is then transmuted into something quite different from what it was in direct face-to-face situations.

The folk scene, and the folk clubs especially, are in a very special and ambivalent role with regard to these forms of dominant musical socialisation. In some ways they are countering them, in a very specialised way, to set up new (or new forms of old) modes of listening consciousness. This is worked out through the special means of staging folk performances, and the role of acoustic, unamplified music within the genre. It is also connected with the forms of disruption that the folk scene actively encourages, but which, I am going to argue, are permitted within only very specialised and attenuated circumstances.

If in our society musical performance as a part of people's active social life is not common, if live music tends towards either the background or the concert, then the folk scene is in a very special position. At the same folk club to which I had taken my friend there was another occasion when another friend of mine, this time a long-standing folk club attender, got into a similar argument. She had also been asked to be quiet and, in discussion with me, claimed that she expects to be able to talk at the folk club – to talk through the performance.

The discussion aroused considerable indignation in some others present. One argument put to me was that to talk through a song would be like talking 'through' someone when they were conversing with you. At this folk club it was quite common for there to be a 'shhh' from someone during the performance, and it occurred to me that this was due to a certain lack of normative cohesion, from a divergence of expectations with regard to the nature of the musical performance and of the performance setting itself.

This occurred far less at what I would term the 'cosier' folk clubs such as Chelmsford, and it is worth noting that the interchange between performer and audience in the form of chorus singing and heckling is more prevalent at this type of club. The Chelmsford club has socialised its audience into active participation and in so doing has structured a new form of performer–audience interchange, one which is informal, yet attentive, though not overly demanding of that attention. They have removed the background effect.

In the folk clubs 'structured informality', the articulation of apparent informality, is tightly bound by a series of mores and expectations as to how to behave. At Chelmsford the audience is integrated into the performance to create one social event (as opposed to lots of little ones, as occurs when people talk in little groups). As such it appears the more relaxed of the two clubs, and the more informal, but only because of the greater normative cohesion with regard to expectations of behaviour. It might appear less formal, but it is the more tightly bound by its own rule-governed behaviour.

At the former club, which is far more likely to have people chatting at the bar or in small groups, there is less of a feeling of unity in the occasion, more of a distancing of audience and performer, which this necessarily creates, though it is important to note that here the bar is in the room, whereas at Chelmsford it is in a separate room. The lack of a bar in the room may be an important factor. Many performers and club organisers prefer folk clubs not to have the bar in the room, and clubs such as Chelmsford have made a conscious effort to find premises without an internal bar. This was true of the former club, too, but they had difficulty in finding suitable premises. Certainly the presence of the bar may be one key feature in distinguishing the different performance aesthetics of these two clubs, in that it might then be more difficult for club members to socialise new members into the mores of the folk scene, given that the onus is to preserve the appearance of informality. This relates to my claim that 'cosiness' is accomplished through inculcating the appropriate mores of behaviour. At clubs such as Chelmsford the cosiness belies a careful and conscious deconstruction of staging. The creation of inclusivity is such as to destroy the distancing inherent in performing. The raucous chorus singing, the cat-calls, insults, juxtaposition of floor singers with paid performers, lack of a dressing room for performers, lack of conductors and the lack of glamour are all constructed for a given end. When this succeeds, when a folk club audience does go quiet in rapt attention, it is going quiet for a very different reason from a classical music audience. The rapt attention is not a given precondition:

> That's the joy of the folk scene – that you're judged on pure real-time performance... but as a performer there is no possible greater indication of respect than an audience being pin-drop silent. Clapping applause is Pavlovian. That's the greatest approval a performer can get.

As we can see from these comments from a professional folk singer, 'pin-drop' silence is desired, but it acquires its special significance precisely from the fact that it is not overtly demanded. However, since the structuring and layout of the musical event do not clearly demonstrate to the uninitiated the appropriate form of audience behaviour, this can then be misunderstood by those not socialised into this performance setting. Informality is actively created in order to appear natural when it is in fact elaborately contrived. It is because certain moments do not seem contrived that they can engender a special tension, as when an audience falls 'pin-drop silent'.

In far smaller social settings not diffused with the 'background effect' I would suspect that such a dynamic mood range would have been natural. It might be the diffusion of the background effect which has restructured musical consciousness to prevent informal, communicative yet relaxed music-making. This would tie in with a lot of other factors, not the least of which being that in Western society people no longer generally expect to make music as part of everyday normal social interaction (Bennett 1980). The mode of listening particular to the folk scene is no longer a societal norm.

Because relaxedness no longer predisposes towards partaking in music-making, and now generally exists in contrast to listening which is associated with the concert, then its re-creation requires not only the careful establishment of the parameters within which it might happen, but also that audience's expectations have to change; they have to be resocialised. A folk audience is not just an audience that likes folk music; it is an audience which listens in a different way. What has been revived is not just a sound form, but also associated modes of behaviour, although in a very different social context.

To restructure attentive listening, but to set it in a convivial relaxed framework, is to attempt to contrive something that is socially complex. It is far easier to seek to structure and impose listening in a setting redolent of formality and stricture. Didactic modes of communication are imposed upon us from an early age at school, and are associated with a hierarchical configuration of power relations. But to make a musical event feel relaxed and informal is to restructure the way in which the performers are regarded. Because of the intrusion of the dominant socio-musical aesthetic this is even to admit the likelihood of the destruction of the special features of the musical event. To maintain face-to-face contact via such means as low volume and the location of events in pubs and bars is to open up the possibility of the destruction of the performance, and yet this rarely happens. This is because of an elaborate construction of informality which occurs in the folk scene.

A very conscious destaging and destruction of glamour occurs to maintain the face-to-face intercommunicative nature of musical performance. This occurs in very informal settings, but settings which are elaborately set up and structured to contain the events. Folk events are not in the form of 'anything goes' or 'free-for-alls', and contain within them elaborate means of maintaining their own core socio-musical aesthetic and ethos.

Some particularly interesting examples of destaging occurred at Keith Festival, a festival run by the Traditional Music and Song Association [of Scotland] (TMSA), an organisation devoted to preserving and promoting traditional song and music.

The TMSA was founded in 1967 and thus is contrasted to its English cousin, the English Folk Song and Dance Society, as being a product of the 'second', as opposed to the 'first', folk revival. Oddly, although a product of the folk revival, the TMSA regarded itself as being somewhat at odds with the folk scene which it considered to be dominated by 'revivalists'. The TMSA almost exclusively sought to give a platform to source singers, that is, those who had learned their music directly from the folk tradition in their own families and communities. It sought to give the tradition bearers a platform to enable their songs and music to reach a wider audience.

A difficulty presented itself in structuring such events to retain the essential informality which would normally have surrounded these singers' and musicians' 'performances', though that is not to say that this issue was always confronted overtly. Source singers were far from being concert musicians, and most were quite unused to performing in a concert setting, or to bodies of people whom they did not know personally.

The TMSA has evolved many interesting institutions to manage the staging of informality, and throughout the festival the essential tussle between staging and informality, a central tension of the whole folk scene, was demonstrated in many ways. Many of these strategies might not even have been apparent to the performers concerned.

The almost total concentration by the TMSA on source singers in itself imposed a sort of structure upon the official events. The adulation of the source singers meant that those who had come up through the revival could not achieve the same status as was the case early on in the folk revival in England. In TMSA festivals this was reinforced by the fact that revival performers were rarely booked. Even as this policy mellowed in later years it established the principle that those who had prior knowledge of, and access to 'source' material were placed in a high-status position.

Furthermore, through this policy the TMSA was resisting the build-up of professionalism which was entering the English folk scene with the rise of touring professionals and semi-professionals. The revivalists who were associated with the TMSA had a much more established model to follow than in England, and there was not such a separation of source and traditional singers from the revivalists. This might seem a contradiction given that I have stated that revival singers were not booked to any great extent by the TMSA, at least in its early years. However, the TMSA festivals were extremely popular amongst revivalists, and the higher exposure which source singers thus gained in Scotland than in England ensured the fostering of closer links.

This had an immediate effect upon the nature of folk events. For a start, there was not the same consciousness of revival. While this may have been more so in the minds of committee members and organisers, the involvement of source singers and musicians who were more closely identified with their own local communities led to an identification more with the terms 'Scottish' and 'traditional' music than with the term and concept of 'folk' music. In Scotland even today there remains a far greater degree of separation of these terms than in England, and, especially in many rural districts, folk music normally means something quite different than traditional music and is associated with guitars and singalong music, the image presented in the media of the English folk revival of the 1960s. Thus the TMSA festival at Keith is known as Keith Festival, not Keith Folk Festival, and has evolved as a community festival but with a high concentration on traditional music. The festival has a high degree of support locally, and the influx of 'folkies' is subsumed within the far greater number of local people present.

The mainstay of the official events is a series of eight 'ceilidhs'. These are a form of concert presentation where the mechanisms of informality are stretched as far as possible while still retaining the overall cohesion and continuity of the event. A bare minimum of formal structural constraints ensures the coherence and integrity of the performance. At these ceilidhs the performers sing and play to seated audiences, but they are deliberately constituted quite differently from concerts. Elements of destaging and informality are built into them in many ways. A key factor is the layout. The Seafield ceilidh, for instance, was held in a largish long hall. Four long rows of trestle tables were placed the length of the hall parallel to the sides of the walls. This broke the tendency towards rows of seats redolent of concerts. Everyone sat side-on, and the hall became a series of eight long columns with a few people standing at the bar, which was situated in an alcove along one side of a wall.

In another ceilidh in the Plough Inn there was an almost complete absence of staging as it would be normally understood. The stage, a very small raised wooden board, was placed directly adjacent to the toilets. The room itself was small and crushed due to the number of people crammed into it, such that it was almost physically impossible to maintain the separation of musician and performer. People were brushing past the performers to get to the toilet, and the next performer had to squeeze through the standing audience to get in. Yet in this atmosphere, smoky, with the drink flowing, with much friendly pushing and shoving generated by people who were entering or leaving or going to the bar or the toilet, there was almost complete silence for the performer while singing, yet there was no obvious person acting to create order or any calls of 'shhh'. This was because the audience wanted the event to feel informal.

These two ceilidhs presented an atmosphere of informality, but it also appeared to me that there was also a tight, although almost imperceptible structure. Something was holding these events together. The audiences were paying attention, but without a highly stylised formality. The informality was not acting to destroy the integrity of the performance as performance, although this did occasionally happen, in circumstances I will come to.

The festival did include a couple of main concerts and organisationally it would have seemed simplest to have put a lot more people into concert-type venues. Although the festival did have a concert on each night, the mainstay of the festival was the series of ceilidhs. The artists had to tour the venues presenting short twenty-minute spots so that all guests appeared at all venues. The effect was to give the feeling of a series of small social gatherings, yet the festival as a whole was large. The guests had to travel from ceilidh to ceilidh most of the evening. This was exhausting for the guests and presented severe organisational problems.

Such an elaborate attempt to create informality required a high degree of coordination on the part of the organisers. At each event throughout the town the organisers maintained contact through the use of intercom private radios to ensure that each ceilidh was supplied with a guest, and to coordinate the timing of spots. Organisers with intercoms periodically came into the ceilidhs and winked to the MCs to ensure the coordination and timing of guest spots. This was a very deliberate attempt to circumvent the staging of large events. Quite such a deliberate attempt to avoid the large concert format as occurred here was perhaps extreme, but I found considerable irony in the fact that an attempt to become informal in fact required the elaboration of considerable artifice.

The short timing of concert spots had the effect of interrupting the build-up and peaking of guests' performances, and prevented adulation of any one performer. No one could then have top billing. The programming happened according to who was where at any given moment and thus who finished off at any one concert became random. This served to prevent a pecking order establishing between guests, and the short timing of spots was more appropriate to people who knew a few songs or tunes, rather than those who would elaborately construct 'a performance' of a longer duration.

TMSA festivals are unusual in comparison to most folk festivals in that they do not pay guests, providing them instead with board and lodging only. This policy arose from the stated aim of the TMSA of providing source singers with a platform. Opposition to the professionalisation of the folk scene as it was developing elsewhere led to a deliberate 'no fee' policy in which only expenses are paid. Although revivalists are now booked for TMSA festivals they still do not receive fees. This powerfully changes the relationship of the guest to the audience. Frequently professional and semi-professional singers will agree to perform at TMSA festivals such as Keith but then this becomes a 'let-your-hair-down' type of performance. When a performer such as Aly Bain, who is internationally known and can command large fees, plays at Keith, the fact that he is not commanding a large fee is thus known and colours the performance itself. He fools around a lot, and he will readily play unrehearsed with other musicians, and the resulting relaxation in professional presentation is readily soaked up by the audience. Goffman (1974) indicates how important the back room is to all forms of staging. In musical performance the back room is part of the elaboration of mystique when performers exit from a stage door and are only visible in performance. This was quite different at this particular ceilidh, as it is at almost all folk scene events. There was no back room. On this occasion, when not playing Aly Bain just stood at the bar as would anybody else. In the folk scene it thus becomes very difficult to put on a 'front' because it is almost impossible to get outwith the public eye. But on so many occasions, as at this one, the performers made no attempt to do so.

Street life forms an essential element of Keith Festival, with music in the bars, on the pavement, almost literally everywhere. However, even here it is not a case of anything goes. A large number of youths are attracted by the camaraderie and street activities, including street drinking and the ready availability of alcohol. Although there is not much trouble to speak of, much of the informal street music-making is in fact inhibited by the sheer number of youths present. Informality of this type is greatly resented by the concert and session attenders because it interferes with the music-making.

But I did observe one 'interference' with a programmed event at Keith Festival which occurred in such a way that it was not resented. One particularly prevalent feature of the festival is the juxtaposition or close proximity of formal and informal events. At the Ashley Lodge Hotel which housed one of the programmed ceilidhs the informality of the official event had been pushed to an extreme degree. It was the smallest of the circuit of ceilidhs at the festival, with a capacity of only about twenty-five people. The number of people in the room filled it without too much of a crushing. People arranged themselves to face into the centre of the room and guests who came in performed from what ever part of the room they could best find a space. The MC announced from the small space in the middle of the room and then went and sat back down in his seat. Because this official event had been deliberately 'staged' to maximise informality within the limitations of maintaining it as a coherent event it raised the danger, if that is the right word, of it being identified as being 'truly' informal.

Now truly informal musical events at folk festivals have quite a different 'trajectory' than official events. An official event is programmed for a given period of time, and other than with perhaps a late start will conform to this. An informal event, such as a session or singaround, is not programmed to any time period whatsoever. It has to sustain itself and if it loses momentum it will cease. During the course of a festival many sessions come and go, and it is rare for one to keep on going for many hours. Generally their intensity rises and wanes and, depending on the time of day, they will normally have one or a couple of cycles of intensity. Only for a relatively short period will they have their maximum 'energy level' – to be measured perhaps by numbers participating, frequency of items performed and degree of attention paid in the room.

Thus I was quite surprised to observe the official Ashley Lodge ceilidh beginning to merge with the session which was taking place informally in the adjoining room. This was because it now appeared that the integrity of the musical event was threatened. This adjoining session was well attended and the throng of people attending spilled over into the corridor, leaving the door open. The intrusion of the adjoining session interfered with the ceilidh, but instead of any complaints the official event was subverted by the close proximity and intrusion of the unofficial one and the two events became one. No one seemed to mind. Everyone appeared happy and there were plenty of comments as to its having been a good night. The compère himself did not speak of it as a disaster – it was almost as if this sort of unofficial take-over was a welcomed event. The spiritedness of the music-making seemed testimony to that.

This was an example of the demarcation of type of event having been made deliberately tentative. In this instance the event had been formally staged in such a manner that it could be easily subsumed into an informal event which 'encroached' upon it. This is not to say that the event could easily have been subverted into some other type of event leading to its destruction as a musical event, and it would be a mistake to assume that the appearance of informality is such as to mean that the event is less tightly structured and not having clear defining boundaries. This was a good example of how rules can have tentative elements built into them. In this case it was the boundary of the event itself which was allowed to be tentative rather than the coherence of the event. If the challenge had come from something which would have subverted the ceilidh's purpose to perform traditional music I suspect that the outcome would have been different and the programmed ceilidh would have continued.

The major English folk festival at Sidmouth provided some odd contrasts with regard to staging and informality. For this, the flagship of the English festivals, the organisers put on numerous events at different venues which were slick and polished, but at the festival as a whole there were a range of different events of very different 'informality' levels.

Humour was often deliberately employed to break down the staging. At one concert in the rather uncomfortable venue mentioned in the last chapter there were several highly talented musicians. Just before the first of these was about to play, the MC commented: 'And now we'll have some really boring musicians playing all the flash.' I became acutely aware that this served a function beyond that of being merely a funny comment. It served to prevent undue focus upon the musicians' undoubted skill and in so doing subverted adulation. To adulate is to set up distance, to stage. Just as at Keith, many devices were being employed to destage. A lack of comfort, an atmosphere of heat and pressed bodies was one, and on more than one occasion I overheard a discussion of the merits of the festival which included the comment 'and if this is what they do to their friends . . .'

The only alternative to the above event for anyone wanting to listen to the festival guest singers and musicians was a concert put on in a local cinema. Despite being capable of holding many more people it was by far the lesser of the two in terms of popularity. A comment in the festival newsletter described it thus:

> The Radway Cinema turned out to be a pleasant hall, with reasonable acoustics, if a little formal. Because the bar is small and in the cinema foyer, it doesn't allow for a lot of socialising and on top of that the artists are segregated off backstage.

So these elements are consciously noted. In the Radway I was particularly interested to note that even here, in the most staged event of all, the house lights remained on during the whole performance – there was still that subversive attempt to destage.

A key feature in folk music is for the central sociability of the music to remain paramount. One accomplished folk singer remarked to me at this festival that:

> The crack is essential; just listening to good music all night, you'd get bored – you need the crack.

Several respondents made a similar point. Here is an Aberdeen folk club floor singer:

> *NLM*: What makes a good night at the folk club?
> *P*: The total atmosphere of the place. The quality of the guest and the floor singers, the humour and the response of the audience around. All those elements have got to be present. I've seen nights where the artist has been an excellent musician but that's all he has been. Technically he's been good but that's all . . .

At Sidmouth the crack, the exchange of insults and so forth served to add a tension. As a destaging device it was also accompanied by many others. For instance, the performers had to climb over the audience to reach the stage. The MCs were scruffy. Both the MCs and the performers carried pints of beer up on to the stage with them, often singing while they were holding their glass. My own summing up of the song events at this festival would be with the term 'unglamourous'.

The director of the English Folk Dance and Song Society had been doing much work to promote the interests of the folk scene within the media and the Arts Council. I asked him whether he is ever embarrassed to talk to the Arts Council about folk music:

> Yes. Terrible. Because these people won't understand it. These people are used to going to a theatre where there is a lavatory which is clean; where they can have a wee before they go in; where they can stand quietly at the bar and have a nice G and T [gin and tonic] and then go and sit in a proper seat and the performance starts five minutes dead after the advertised time; the interval will happen on time. These are the conventions they are used to. I can't take someone like that into a folk club.

One particular feature of the folk scene which should be bracketed with destaging is the existence of the floor singer. Virtually all folk clubs have a part of the evening devoted to floor spots where people from the audience get up to perform. This, probably more than any other single feature, prevents a concert-type atmosphere. The variation of standards and the resulting unpredictability itself sets up a tension. The phenomenon of the floor singer prevents the adulation and fetishisation of quality. The very best folk performers have to perform at events where sometimes quite dire floor performers have immediately preceded them. However, while many performers might themselves wish more adulation and concert-type staging, this one feature serves to destroy any such pretensions on the part of performers. Certainly I noted that it was the slickest performers who expressed the most dislike of floor performers. Performance by floor singers at folk clubs also serves to minimise social distance in another way. Probably more than in any other musical genre, novices are not separated off from more experienced performers and the institution of the floor singer serves to train novice performers. This does not occur through a hierarchy of gigs with novices performing at lesser gigs as in other musical genres. Novice performers are given the opportunity of performing at mainstream events. This also has the effect of allowing novice performers to perform without having to set up their own gigs. It must be quite a step for a new performer to gain a first outlet in a full gig, yet there is no intermediate stage in, say, rock or classical music, as there is in the British folk scene.

Bennett (1980), talking of 'garage rock', indicates that finding venues for new musicians is far more problematic. Early exposure to audiences requires being booked as a fully functioning band. This indicates that musical training is either privatised (in the garage), or becomes subject to formal education (as in classical music). Without ready access to truly informal outlets for music-making, musicians in modern Western society have few outlets. The existence of the phenomenon of the floor singer in the folk scene must be therefore be seen as a special case. In consequence the folk music movement has acted as a training ground for performers of all types. Many household names in rock music, cabaret and comedy, including people like Paul Simon, Barbara Dickson, Pam Ayres, Jasper Carrott and Billy Connolly, started off in folk clubs. Not surprisingly, for those performers who have stayed with the folk scene, the institution of the floor singer/musician arouses very ambivalent feelings. I spoke to Paul James of Blowzabella, a semi-professional English instrumental folk band:

> *NLM*: Do you like performing along with floor performers?
> *P*: Yes and no. When I was sixteen I used to go to this folk club in Reading and it did a lot for me 'cause I was able to get up there and make a complete idiot of myself and learn so much about 'learning to be a performer'. It was brilliant but the trouble is now you have to put up with that process yourself. [*Laughs*] I'm totally sympathetic towards it personally, except in some circumstances . . . it depends on the club.

Most professional and semi-professional folk musicians in my survey expressed satisfaction with the idea of having floor spots, but with certain reservations that something should be done to ensure a certain quality of performance on their part. The other main complaint was that the floor singers took up too great a part of the evening. I asked one American folk singer touring British folk clubs whether he liked performing along with the floor singers:

> *D*: Oh yes. It's a way of warming things up and they [the floor singers] feel they are part of it. But sometimes they put on six or seven people . . .

The guest spot had been shortened at Chelmsford folk club on one of the nights I visited. I asked the guest, Paul James, about this:

> At Chelmsford there were quite a lot of people who'd come to see us especially who wouldn't come to that club on a regular basis. And they'd paid their money to get in and we ended up playing two thirty-minute sets. We could just as easily have done two forty-five-minute sets. But these people had to listen to a lot of people that they didn't want to and only get two half-hour spots from us. This is very common and you hear this from everyone – getting value for money.

This was a common occurrence but one rarely commented upon by club organisers. I suspect that this cannot be put down to incompetence or amateurism, as is so often claimed, but must be seen as a deliberate if non-articulated feature. It is a tension which is inherent and derives from tendencies which are pushing in different directions. Whatever socio-musical aesthetic the folk scene tries to structure for itself it has to do this within a wider musical context. Folk performers have access to ready reference models outside the folk scene in addition to frequent experience of actually playing outwith it. As booked performers they are unlikely to find the equivalent of the floor performer outside the folk scene and it is not surprising that this sets up countervailing pressures.

Thus we find comments relating, for instance, to notions of value for money. But for many clubs the floor spots are more than 'warm-up' spots and it is the informal performance by known people which makes the atmosphere of the club night and which makes it a 'club' as such. In the early days of the folk scene, guest performances were rare and it was the performance by residents or floor singers which provided the central *raison d'être* for the club's existence. Today, although evenings with a guest performer tend to be the norm, the addition of booked guests brings variety and talent, adding interest and week-to-week variety, but it may not be the central reason for the club performance itself, which may indeed still be the floor singers and those features of the very club atmosphere and structure which serve to mark it off from being a weekly concert. This then would fit in with truncated guest spots where the guest's performance time is cut short to make room for the number of local floor performers. An informal, do-it-yourself ethos in music-making may also associate with this feature, serving to depress the status of the booked performer and prevent tendencies towards star status and adulation of these performers. No wonder that they sometimes resent it.

There is a perennial discussion of what to do about truly dire performances in the folk scene, but it should be stressed that a great many floor performances vary from the competent to the excellent, even the virtuosic, which is not surprising for a musical genre which celebrates active musical participation and downplays the professionalisation of its music. The fact that floor performers get ample opportunities to perform serves to enhance their performing ability. Since fame and fortune are not to be found to any great extent in the folk scene, it is unlikely that novice performers would be willing to undergo the same deprivations that inspire so many other unsuccessful musicians in other scenes.

Folk audiences do appreciate quality and talent but they do not seem to demand nor even expect it. Sometimes they can appear very undiscriminating, a comment I have heard mentioned in a deprecating way by many musicians not familiar with the folk scene who have come into contact with it. I have heard it asked many times why folk audiences put up with such bad performances. I came to realise that sometimes this goes even further, and the folk audiences themselves do not seem to mind. Certainly this is supported by the findings of the folk club audience questionnaire. Of the five propositions relating to floor singer standards presented, only 3 per cent supported the proposition that 'The folk club should ensure much higher standards of performance from floor performers' and yet only 12 per cent supported the proposition that 'There is nothing wrong with the general standard of floor performers'.

Chelmsford folk club is widely regarded locally as a good folk club, yet it evidenced a marked variability of standards. On one club night the guests, Joe and Antoinette McKenna, were of a particularly virtuosic standard. The floor spots were varied: there were some who were of touring standard (and they were in such bands) and there were a couple who could hardly sing and who forgot their lines. As I was leaving the organiser commented to me that it had been a very good evening. I asked whether these two performances had not spoiled it and I was told not at all, that this was just to be expected of a folk club night. This variability of standards was quite accepted.

I suspect there are reasons for this acceptance. A variation of standards goes together with the relaxed atmosphere which folk clubs try to foster. It prevents a stultified atmosphere, but aesthetically these performances are tolerated because they serve as a contrast; not specifically because they are 'bad' but because they represent inexperience, which accords with an ethos of encouraging participation and the nurturing of active musical involvement. But they also serve a counter-function to highlight moments when the audience is utterly and totally drawn in by a virtuosic performance. Instead of an atmosphere of reverence permeating the whole night, an atmosphere of informality is set up. This could easily be misconstrued as akin to a pub gig where chatter is permitted at any time during a performance. At a folk club the chatter, the aspects of informality, must be within bounds. The relaxed atmosphere and poor standards serve to mark off and accentuate the high spots when they occur. When they do occur they are then perceived as being spontaneous and unexpected. By being neither demanded nor expected on any particular occasion this provides the 'high spots' with a special significance which persistent reverence or persistent irreverence on the part of audiences would dismantle.

Both of these models of audience behaviour are widely misunderstood on the folk scene, again because of the symbolic ambiguity. If the symbolic role of relaxedness and incompetence were too overtly formalised in order to highlight good performances then this would have the air of artifice and deny spontaneity. Thus many members of a folk audience often complain about the informality, chatter, noise from the bar, people getting up to buy drinks during the performance, and so on. Others complain because they have to be quiet during songs and find the atmosphere rigid and imposing. This ambivalence is set up precisely because a folk club is not a formal concert or a pub gig. As symbolic markers these trappings serve key functions, but they are also open to misinterpretation which can itself serve to underline a certain air of the unknown and the unexpected in the structuring of the musical event.

In this sense it is true to say that folk audiences are highly sensitised and socialised, to a finely tuned and well-honed degree, with regard to the limits of behaviour at a folk club. It is scarcely surprising that the folk clubs generate such heated argument as to artistic purpose, performing standards, aesthetic criteria and so on. But the fine line between anarchy and rigidity has to be maintained in subtle ways. Too much irreverence, or indeed too little, and the folk club becomes something else, a weekly concert, a privately run pub gig or whatever.

The existence of the floor singer, then, powerfully restructures the very nature of the performance. Floor singers take away artistic control of the mood and patterning of a whole night. They are quite at odds with 'support acts' whose function is precisely that – to support. Floor singers are the club's own portion of an evening. They insert an element into the evening that is not professional in the direct sense of not relying on payment. Some of the more 'polished' performers particularly resent the power that floor singers wield. However, others are more tolerant and recognise the direct access that the institution of the floor singer gave them personally in learning their trade as folk musicians. Here is John Skelton of the House Band:

> *J*: The thing I like about the folk scene is the way we all got started. The fact that anybody can go along and play usually. But it's a double-edged thing. It can be very good because it's the only sort of music where people can get up and play in front of an audience really other than sitting in the corner of a bar or something, but it works both ways because it's not discriminating in any way. We've all been floor singers in our time.
>
> *NLM*: Do you find it's an important way of learning your stage skills?
>
> *J*: Yes – without realising it at the time.

I found that the commonest reaction on the part of professional singers was one of guarded acceptance. I asked Tich Frier, a full-time professional folk singer of over twenty years' standing, whether he liked the set-up of performing along with floor performers.

> *T*: It depends on the floor performers. If they are crap and I get embarrassed I hate it. If you can see the club organiser scrabbling around for people to sing then you start to worry. Because if they are bad the audience are not going to be in a good mood ... floor singers don't think of it as being there to warm

things up for the guest. In fact on most occasions they are there to cool things down for the guest and it means you have got to work twice as hard. But most folk clubs are trapped into that silly wee formula – floor spots, guest does half an hour, floor spots, guest does half an hour, which isn't long enough I think. Certainly not if the floor singers are bad.

NLM: Are they quite happy about that sometimes?

T: It depends. Some people have funny attitudes. They'll apologise to you because you've only done twenty minutes in the last set but they put on five or six floor singers.

The booked performer occupies the same performance space as a novice, separated in time perhaps by only a few seconds. The folk clubs almost always put on a guest straight after floor performers. Although they have an interval the normal pattern is to start the first half with floor performers followed by the guest, and to repeat the same in the second half. The floor performers also serve to add spontaneity. The audience literally does not know what it is going to get. Frequently floor performances can be very good, and when this occurs it will be talked about for weeks. Clubs seem to take a special pride in the fact that performances every bit as good as those of booked guests can and do come from unpaid floor singers. Bryan Martin, chairman of the Hoy at Anchor folk club, remarked:

> Some casual floor singers dislike our club. I suspect that's because the average standard of floor spots is very high as folk clubs go and even guests will be slightly unnerved just by that. They'll hear Kitty or Steve and then they're going to go on and sing and play the guitar and think 'I am no better than that'. I had a box player sidle up to me – booked guest – who said: 'Is Redman here tonight? Thank Christ for that.'

Many folk performers quite consciously attempt to preserve the performance structure of a more intimate and informal event. Here is Ian MacCalman of The MacCalmans:

> *NLM*: If you were playing to a club with a strong traditional ethos you'd probably tailor your performance to the club more than you would at His Majesty's Theatre?
>
> *I*: Last night we almost went overboard trying to tailor His Majesty's audience to a kind of folk club. We try to get an atmosphere in a folk club, we find that if we're talking too slick or we're appearing too slick then it's too slick for us and we'll deliberately find a song that we don't really know very well or say things just to throw the other two just to get that informal bit . . .
> Another interesting point is you'd be chucked out of a theatre company or anything if you were seen anywhere near the theatre bar before the show. We do that deliberately to show there is no 'us up on the stage and them down there' to try and get that the clubby bit. I'd say the stupidist things on stage just to get a reaction.

For those not socialised into the mores of the folk scene it would be easy to misconstrue features of the informality presented by folk clubs and to adopt behaviour more appropriate to the musical forms which it closely resembles. However, on the odd occasion the underlying rules are laid bare. I had attended a folk club in the North-East of England. This appeared to me a good club, with chorus singing, heckling, humour; it had an air of dynamism, it was a club and not just a live music venue. The guest was Jim Eldon. Jim is one of the very best traditionally oriented performers, who makes the songs live and puts them together with stories in such a way that his whole spot seems to be saying something rather than simply entertaining. These songs are communicated with the sort of directness as recorded in descriptions of performers from the folk tradition. It made me realise how, in contrast to Jim, many very good folk revival performers perform their material in a disembodied way – an academic type of approach that fetishises the 'past-ness' of the songs – the singer had learned this from so-and-so, from this or that collection and this is X's or Y's version. Jim's performance was quite unlike this.

The club itself appeared odd. There were people dressed up in a way that said that this wasn't a genre or an interest group but a village night out. It was definitely a 'good time' night and the audience was lapping him up, often with raucous out-of-tune singalongs which added much to the atmosphere and stripped it of artistic pretension. But a very key and telling thing happened this night. The club was particularly jovial with a very strong tinge of the informal, with good reciprocal banter between the guest and the audience, cackling laughter and so on. Some of this was rowdy, with interjections on the part of the audience being made in quite a forceful manner.

The MC got up at one point and said that he was sorry to have to bring in a sour point but there were some people who were showing no respect to the artist by talking during his performance. As he said this the 'culprits' were still not listening and it was only at this point that I was aware of the disturbance that they had been causing. I had been blocking out the background chatter in my concentration upon the performer, as, it then immediately became clear to me, had the majority of the audience who had been actively partaking in the performance in terms of attentiveness, banter, chorus singing and so on. I had just taken the informality and the hum of background noise as 'normal' and bound in with the informal nature of the proceedings. However, the intrusion of the MC made me realise that this surface 'reading' of the event was quite wrong. As the MC was castigating the noise makers in a general fashion – I should point out that they were not being overly rowdy, just inattentive and talking quietly – he then pounced on the small group who had still not heard and said 'And I'm talking to you!' in a very loud, unfriendly tone. The room went very silent and this group then looked extremely embarrassed. The MC delivered a short homily to the effect that those listening should give respect to the singers.

At this point I presumed that the MC had greatly overstepped the mark in breaking the mores surrounding the structuring of the event, and that this would alter the tone of the night. I had the view that this would embarrass the audience, too, and end the informal jocular nature of the evening. What so surprised me was that when the MC started taking certain members of the audience to task, initially in an anonymous way, it was not those who were being rowdy and interjecting that he was focusing on. This was not the nature of the disruption. Those who were castigated were those who had withdrawn from the musical event to create their own social space within the performance frame and who were having their own conversations in what seemed to me to be quite an unobtrusive manner. It was this group who were regarded as disruptive and threatening to the coherence of the event. I would take some corroborative evidence from the audience reaction which was supportive of the MC. To my surprise the audience clapped the MC and continued in the same boisterous vein once the intercession was passed. The evening carried on as if nothing had happened but without the aforementioned background murmur. It was smoothed over immediately by Jim Eldon who made a joke when he resumed his performance and that was it. I was myself greatly shocked. The informality that I had been witnessing had appeared to me as reminiscent of an attentive audience at a pub gig. If this had been the case the outcome of this event would have been very different.

Mullen (1983), in his study of public house entertainers, has observed that when a pub entertainer gains the rapt attention of an audience, this is far from being an indication that the performer commands the respect of the audience. In these settings a performance is always very likely to be ignored or heckled. I suspect it is the growth of such a tendency in folk clubs which Martin Carthy is referring too when he expresses his dislike of the 'entertain-me attitude' that he finds so prevalent outwith the folk scene and which is also coming to penetrate within it. In a pub gig a 'high' can be generated when a performer captures an audience and manages to change the performance to being more than background music. In the folk scene this is somewhat different. Respect, or at least politeness, is more pervasive.

In the case of the pub gig, rapt attention provides a buzz through its precariousness, the fact that it is not expected. In the folk scene, a buzz in performance is again not always expected but attention is. It does not matter if this can take the form of interjection or even occasional boisterousness, as long as it is not seen as being threatening to the coherence of the performance. In a sense it is adding to it, since if the threat of challenge, of usurpation or rejection, is removed from the performer's relationship with the audience, then these features of behaviour would serve to reinforce the participatory ethic of the folk scene. In a folk club there tends not to be the precariousness of the structuring of the musical event in the same manner as Mullen (1983) terms the 'impure performance frame of the public house entertainer'. In a folk club the audience is not liable to 'contract out' (Mullen 1983) of the performance as in the case of a pub gig. In a folk club, despite many surface similarities to a pub gig, the underlying structuring of the performance is quite different.

An apparent lack of formality and staging in the folk scene belies the fact that performers do indeed have to construct a careful front, only that in the case of the folk scene the lack of a 'stage door syndrome' can actually mean that the performers get no respite. At a folk festival the front has to be maintained for the duration of the festival and not just for the individual gigs. One semi-professional English folk band member said:

> *R*: People who see me on stage – that's a very little part of me. It's not me. It's
> sometimes very upsetting. They expect me to be bouncing around and why
> aren't I always like that and in fact at Sidmouth it obviously upset somebody
> very much when I didn't switch on the total professional thing. I was over-tired
> and you normally find it somewhere within you to be able to switch it on. There
> was one time when it didn't for part of the gig and someone sent me a little
> anonymous note saying 'what's wrong, because the sparkly Rosy didn't come
> through?'
> *NLM*: Was that eerie?
> *R*: Yes and it was very sad and it made me realise how professional you have got
> to be. You must turn that on. It is a professional musical attribute but it is also
> a protection. But it does rebound against you because people think that you're
> like that all the time . . . At a folk festival you have the face on for most of the
> festival.

The whole festival becomes an extension of the performance. By now I think
the reader will be aware that I regard informality as a problematic concept.
The assertion of informality is about the removal of expectations of behaviour
and these can have quite the opposite effect (and intention). One function of
the high degree of informality in the folk scene is control, control by the
organisers and promoters of the events, and by implication the control of
audiences over performers, since these organisers are not removed from their
audiences by the establishment of distancing through professionalisation.
There may be inbuilt structural reasons why the folk scene did not 'sell out' to
anything like the same degree as, say, punk, reasons which are connected with
why it has not undergone the same faddish rise, crescendo and fall. It may be
a genre which in the context of modern pop culture has a very atypical
trajectory. In my view this is a result of the very specific way the folk scene
has structured and organised itself. The folk club formula of two halves, with a
guest turn and floor performer spots in each half, was a phenomenon which
the British folk scene had created for itself. It certainly did not belong in the
settings of traditional music and it was not imported from the United States.
But it is this formula which has demarcated the performance frame and
thereby set up the particular forms of staging which now characterise the
British folk scene.

Because informality draws the audience into the performance frame this can
cause alarm to those new to the folk scene. An easily drawn conclusion is that
they, as novices or strangers, feel themselves outwith the strongly affirmed
social configuration of the event and can come to feel that its assertion in their
presence must be to demonstrate the existence of a clique. I came to draw this
conclusion from the large number of club committees which claim to be driven
to distraction by this accusation of cliquiness in the act of what they claim is
the creation of informality, even to the point, as in the example of the Hoy at
Anchor folk club, where the demonstration of non-exclusivity was that of an
open invitation to coffee after the club, issued by the MC to all members
of the audience present. But perhaps this feeling is quite natural. It is hardly
natural to have an informal participatory gathering which acts in the
manner of a group of friends on a night out, yet which is staged with certain

elements of a concert structure. The event itself functions as a highly ambivalent symbol.

It is important that the directly interactive informality I am talking about should not be confused with the type of informality associated with easy listening and background music which is the antithesis of music as an inter-active and social medium. The acceptability of talking through a performer in performance derives from mores which are created by 'recording conscious-ness', where the performers are being treated as if they are there to provide recorded music and being regarded as outwith the social frame of the musical event. Kenny Hadden gave an example of such behaviour when describing the worst ever gig of one of the folk bands to which he belongs:

> Two guys who ran the Kirkcaldy folk club asked us to play at some guy's sixteenth birthday party. They couldn't do it so they offered it to us. We went in with a PA which you need for five people. They wanted us to set up on the landing one flight of stairs up, while all the other people were downstairs. You just sort of blank your mind out to these things, we'd been asked to play three half-hours so we'd do it and if somebody comes up and listens, fine, and if not, it's not really our fault. We did that and sure as hell nobody bothered with us at all. People came up and looked. If it had been in a room where people could sit and listen, it might have been different. If you feel you are wasting your time they are not really wanting to listen and you are wasting their time as well.
>
> The worst of it was when the guy came up and two guys went past us, went into one of the bedrooms carrying a record player and set it up half way down the stairs, politely waited until we were finished the set of tunes we were on and then turned on the disco music. We hadn't finished and that annoyed us as they didn't even have the decency to say 'Well, thanks very much but we're going to put this on'. They just did it without asking us.

This behaviour had appalled this band. Folk musicians are very uncom-fortable when put into the role of background music, and the music does not work when placed in an informal setting of this nature, where it is expected to provide a sonic backdrop. In this instance the musicians were disheartened from the start. A superficial appearance of informality also throws the novice at the folk event because at times there will be an intense silence deriving from involvement in the performance on the part of the audience. This is what Martin Carthy was getting at when he stated that he demands involvement on the part of an audience. But to the novice such intensity on the part of an audience in an intimate setting can seem oppressive.

Despite the celebration of informality which runs like a thread through the scene, many artists take their music and its presentation very seriously. Certainly the centrality of informality has presented problems such as the following, described by a professional folk band member:

> *A*: In the mid-1970s Irish and Scottish music almost became as popular as rock music over in Germany and a lot of people took advantage of it and you'd get lots of Irish and Scottish guys going over there, forming a band, getting a few gigs and getting drunk on stage and stuff and it ruined the scene for a lot of other bands.
>
> *NLM*: So you have quite a professional attitude?

A: You have to. We view ourselves as a professional band, we do a professional
show, we carry ourselves in a professional manner. We look after our instruments, we look after our sound system, we look after ourselves.

This is the sort of attitude which is now typical of the touring folk performers
of the 1980s, in itself perhaps something of an irony given the central position
of informality within the genre.

I now present some conclusions I have formed relating to the function of
informality and the staging of formal events in the folk scene.

The backroom is very important to the professionalisation of music since it
allows elaborate construction of staging and performance. In the folk scene the
staging is laid bare. The music of the source singers was not performed in a
setting of stage dressing rooms but at community/family events. Out of this
has come something which continued in the revival, the ethos that folk music
is 'doing' music, that is, that all practitioners can do it, and that in doing it,
and in learning how to do it, they are not separated off from more established
practitioners. Such an ethos not only serves to facilitate learning and therefore
helps generate a large community of performers, but also restructures the
nature of musical events themselves. The central position of inclusivity leads
to the formation of a high tolerance of less talented performers at mainstream
events. Musical apprenticeship occurs in the mainstream events themselves,
which has the effect of establishing an expectation of poor performance among
good. This can have two effects: it can makes the 'good' stand out, but it can
also prevent the elaborate construction of a 'staged' atmosphere. Since the
main spot of the senior artist is then not set in the context of an elaborate
build-up, it is perhaps scarcely surprising that so many professional and semi-
professional artists complain so much about unprofessionalism. But whether
audiences dislike it is not so clear and certainly the questionnaire survey
indicates that this is not the case. Folk audiences are highly tolerant of
variable standards from floor performers. This could be described as one of
the key features of the folk scene and certainly goes a long way to explaining
the low prestige of folk music generally.

The folk scene has thus has stepped outwith some dominant trends in mass
culture. Recording technology and the star system now lead to the expectation
of excellence in musical performance, the presentation of a 'finished article',
which itself represents the increasing commoditisation of musical action.
There are exceptions in the case of certain musical forms, which, like folk
music, have consciously sought to subvert professionalisation and the trend
towards the idealisation of musical performance. Punk stands out as an
example here, but it has articulated this stance in quite a different way,
presenting its challenge to mainstream values in an overt and confrontational
manner.

In the folk scene the subversion of the star syndrome is not accompanied by
any celebration of incompetence, as was certainly the case for a dominant
strand in punk performance. In the folk scene there is a complex interlocution
with informality and variable performing standards. The mixing up of per-

formers of varying standards can have many effects. It subverts staging; it reassociates performing with the process of learning to perform; it creates the perception that the stage is accessible (that anyone, with not too great an effort, is able to become a performer and have the right to the stage); and it associates the performance of the music on the stage with its performance off it. These links are indeed close to the performance context of the traditional music of the British Isles, and leads me to question whether the survival of the folk scene and folk music is not more connected to the form of performance and the nature of the musical event than it is to musical content. This would affect the very criteria for defining folk and traditional music, and point to a definition located in the social meanings of the music.

Certainly a very large proportion of newly composed music is the fare of the folk scene, but it has not lost its contact with the past. The attention paid to style, as opposed to content, must serve to refocus the debate surrounding 'Fakesong' (Harker 1985). The association of the folk revival with a corpus of material from bygone times should be understood in terms other than nostalgia. It demonstrates continuity, and stresses that the songs and the tunes are more than their singers, depressing the presentation of self in folk singing. This is certainly one major difference from the earlier folk revival at the turn of the century, where folk music was collected but arranged in the conventions of classical music. This feature could perhaps be seen as being at the core of the folk scene and certainly comprises a main element of what relates it to the folk tradition. The song is more that the singer. Here is Martin Carthy:

> One of the reasons why Benjamin Britten and Vaughan Williams, their arrangements don't work, is because they are arrangements. The whole thing is freeze-dried and held up – 'look at this: I have brought you the head of Alfredo García' – and what you have got is nothing. It's something that's stopped ... [What] we have [in the revival] is the song in a stage of its development. We have an enormous amount to do with the way it's developed, that's to say, we have changed it. But as far as I am concerned, that song can develop some more. It's not a finished article. I think that the attitude of the people who are listening to the Brittens and the Vaughan Williamses, is that what they are being presented with is a finished polished article, and that's not what I think.

This is not just a very different conceptualisation than that which characterises classical music, whereby compositions are 'fixed' in written manifestation, it is also a reaction against modern popular music where, as Bennett (1980) indicates, the record fixes a given composition in a similar way, and in so doing personalises the song or piece of music, associating it for all time with one individual. If the folk revival has challenged this form of musical consciousness, then this is in itself the strongest link with the folk tradition, far stronger than the preservation of given song texts and melodies, and represents a revival of a feature which powerfully influences the socio-musical aesthetic of the genre, in stark contrast with most other Western music in the late twentieth century. This is inextricably bound into the way the folk scene structures the nature of musical performance through the use of informality.

Informality could thus be described as an organising concept of the folk scene, a quality or an essence which is central to the construction of the musical and social meanings of the performance. What the informality does not demonstrate is a musical form that is merely more loosely structured or less rule-governed than other musical forms. So far I have been largely talking about folk music events that are staged, to the extent that they are programmed to occur at a given time with a given guest performer. But a lot of music in the folk scene is not put on a stage and some of it is indeed truly spontaneous and informal in the sense that the musical event is not formally planned in advance and may or may not even happen. To understand the wider nature of performance in the folk scene, it is important to pay attention to this type of event.

10 The Session

A session is a gathering of musicians who meet informally to play tunes. A singing session or singaround is a similar gathering of singers, though if instrumental and vocal music occur together it is normally referred to as a session. In this chapter I will pay particular attention to the session, outlining elements which indicate its distinct form as a musical event.

A key feature of the session is that the music is played extempore, without written music. The focus is on tunes from the various traditions of the British Isles, normally tunes comprising two parts, each played twice, and eight bars in length.

Structurally, session tunes are usually simple and it is expected that embellishment will be added by the musicians during performance. There are various forms of ornamentation and many of these have a specific terminology. For instance, session musicians refer to a 'roll' where a small preceding note, normally higher in pitch, is added very briefly to a given note, to be followed by a similarly brief additional note, normally lower in pitch, both added without changing the time duration of the 'main' note in relation to the tune as a whole. There are many forms of roll, each of which joins the groups of notes together in a slightly different rhythmic combination. Numerous other devices are employed to render the tune different from its skeletal outline in printed form: the dynamic range may be altered, notes shortened minutely, others lengthened, and others slurred (where a group of notes is played together without separate bowing on a fiddle, or breathing on a flute). These devices are combined together so that a given tune acquires a certain feel and the way in which musicians apply these decorations to tunes gives each session musician a fairly individualistic and distinctive style.

It is important to note that these forms of musical expression occur outwith any written articulation. Many written collections of session tunes have been compiled and are used as a source by session musicians. However, most of these present the tunes in the form of 'bare' notes; it is up to the musicians to provide decoration. This point is often not recognised by musicians coming to folk music from other performance traditions. The misunderstandings on the part of classical musicians who acquire books of session tunes and turn up to join in a session are quite revealing to the structuring ethos of the session, as one session musician explained to me:

> a case in point about a classical musician – I went to Newcastleton [Folk Festival]. There's only two pubs to play in. Sunday I moseyed along to the pub – I thought I'd have a look in because there was a good session there the year before and there was this guy there sitting over in a corner who had been playing with Tony. And Tony will play with anyone, almost, he's a good session man – great repertoire, pissed as a newt, playing with these three people.
>
> Now this guy had his fiddle case open with books of music in front of him and he was playing through the tunes. Now there were some little pointers to this man being not session material. Firstly, he had managed to draw a seat up to a table where his case was in such a way that three places immediately could not be sat upon – there was a whole corner that was excluded from the rest. The pub was quite quiet and . . . was going to fill up. Secondly, he was playing off [written] music – this is not seen or done in sessions. Thirdly, he told everybody else what to play – he would say 'Now we are going to play this' which is also a bad sign. There was this other musician and she couldn't play very well and he had written out chords for her. We sat there munching our tuna fish rolls saying 'What the fuck's going on here?' He was working from Bulmer's [tune book] and he was just working all the way down the page – no repeats or anything. The tunes don't go together, they are not great sets. . . . He just got frozen out of the session.

The confusions mentioned here derive from the relationship of the music in performance to its written representation. Classical musicians cannot readily, by virtue of their training, make sense of those features with which session musicians adorn tunes – rolls, cuts and so on. Within the folk revival the written music does not serve as an aid to performance in performance itself, and this can lead to misinterpretations of appropriate forms of musical action to be adopted within the session setting. The session acquires its significance in real time. The ordering of the tunes is not set out beforehand, the decoration of the tunes is not set out beforehand and the musicians present each play with their own styles and interpretations, thus ensuring that each session acquires certain unique musical characteristics, unique to that particular gathering of session musicians.

It is the interplay of these component elements which creates the special character of a session, as indicated by the comments of another session musician who outlined what for him does and does not dispose in favour of a good session:

> C: At Meigle you tend to have a core of people who go there who play quite a lot of Scottish music and for about two weeks running some other people turned up who don't normally . . . who were very welcome but had an unfortunate habit of worming their way right into the heart of the whole thing and then playing lots of popular Irish reels and so on, not very well. They actually got there earlier. There is a divided area so they could actually take over the section of the pub which normally has the session in it. This fragmented things a bit but it wasn't

clear until about two weeks later when they didn't turn up and when the usual people came in one by one, that there had been no overt agreement that these people had been ruining things, but when everyone came in one by one everyone expressed the same opinion to each other: 'Thank God they're not here this week'. Everyone sat down and had a really great time.

NLM: Could a new person come to session and be quite welcome?

C: Yes. The point is, people do come to the session and are quite welcome, but the people who were coming were getting up people's noses by arriving early and trying to take over as it were. I don't know if they saw that as trying to take over but it certainly fragmented it.

NLM: Could you play those tunes?

C: Yes, but it wasn't really what that session was about in a sense.

NLM: Is there any sort of turn-taking – who instigates a tune going on at a session?

C: Normally there would have been but when they were there that all fell to bits as well. They kept on instigating things. There was a lack of respect for other people present. They don't leave space for other people where normally you would have. If you had a group of people there it would be normal to maybe have a turn around the table at points, but mostly it would be tunes that everybody could join in on.

NLM: So what makes for a really good session?

C: Just, I think, when you have got people with very similar tastes in music all playing together you can get a very satisfactory session. . . .

NLM: So a session doesn't depend upon an audience?

C: Not at all. Like last week in Meigle, in fact for the last two weeks there has not been much of an audience there, but there has been about ten musicians on both nights and it's gone very well.

Since the rules underlying a session are not spelt out in any overt fashion there is always the risk that the coherence of the event can be shattered. An example of such behaviour occurred at a singing session at another folk festival. The disruption was caused by festival goers who were not closely socialised into session etiquette. The singing session was of the type I would label serious (that is to say, not frivolous or light-hearted), and was concentrating on songs from the traditional folk song repertoire.

The entrants walked into the middle of the group of singers and sang light-hearted comedy songs. They did not enter quietly, and on entering took it that the session had not built up to the high point of humour that often accompanies singarounds and sessions. As it happened this was one of those sessions that had risen in intensity to a very serious manner of song rendition, which these entrants had not perceived.

This happening led me to an observation that I then sought to 'test' throughout the festival – that those seeking to participate in a singing session normally slip in quietly. Failure to observe this can shatter the continuity of the singaround. A good singaround or singing session is not a time for hearty welcomes and this type of event should be interpreted in terms not of informality, but of the absence of overt staging.

This singing session was an instance when certain subtle rules were broken. Those entering were made welcome. They were ready to partake in the session, but somehow they transformed it into something else. Certainly this is common in sessions and leads to a general 'ebb and flow' within a session. But the key marker on this session was that the tension or energy level was broken since the singers started to have conversations and one or two went to the bar. The session momentum was reduced and about half an hour after this it broke up, when it had been going for about two hours with no indication whatsoever of waning prior to this.

Earlier on some other people, non-participants, had come into the room, and talked very loudly in close proximity to the singers. But this had not disrupted the energy level. The session continued in an 'intense' manner despite the close proximity of a group of people who were making a fair degree of noise. The key feature was that this group was located outwith the social space of the singing group and their behaviour did not disturb the coherence of the event itself because they were not part of it. They disturbed only to the extent that the noise they were making intruded but they were not interacting with the singers. It was completely different when the second group of participants entered. They had the effect of breaking the coherence of the event.

In a session informality is structured to serve the social configuration of the event. A session, whether instrumental or vocal, is informal only to the extent that the event is not staged. Beyond that it is tightly rule-governed. Even quite unplanned singing sessions can be, and often are, taken very seriously. They can be occasions where singers and musicians give of their best. Neither does informality necessarily dispose towards accessibility. It is sometimes the case that exclusive or semi-exclusive groups set themselves up. The session format can then serve to display this exclusivity in an overt and ostentatious manner. Often the very best musical happenings occur informally and spontaneously and can consequently attract a certain mystique. A good session becomes like the fish that got away. Everyone has heard tell of someone who came across a 'brilliant' session and everyone hopes that they, too, may just happen to be in the right place at the right time. As some of the very best events are not staged – cannot be staged because informality is part of the very essence of what is good about them – then no one can be sure where the next good event is going to be. This destroys the allocation of access to the 'best' events by devices such as high ticket prices and itself serves as part of the structuring ethos of the folk scene. The official high spot at a folk festival is often upstaged, or purported to have been upstaged, by some other event that people go home talking about. Thus informality can serve to highlight events but in an unpredictable manner.

A session is often set up to separate itself from people who are present but not involved in producing music. Although sessions usually take place in public places, normally pubs, session musicians tend to separate themselves to some degree from any public that is present. Sessions gravitate to pubs with small enclosed back rooms or to small bars, and I observed one session establishing itself in an alcove of a lounge bar from where those in the bar could only get a very restricted and incomplete view of the musicians. Although members of the public, friends of the musicians and other people in attendance who could be regarded as a putative audience do listen and may enjoy a session, the session is not focused on these people. The most revealing aspect of session musicians' 'performance' is that the musicians are normally grouped together and face each other so that as they play they are faced inwards towards their fellow musicians rather than outwards to any audience as such.

In some ways this could be understood as the final destruction of performance. People who listen 'happen' to be listening. However, a revealing feature is that a session is usually desired in a setting where other people are present. Few sessions are organised for purely private pleasure, but, and it is a big but, no audience is then sought at the event. Thus it is not strictly performance at all. It certainly is, and is intended to be, the antithesis of staging and for this reason it might be better to talk of 'musical action' in place of the wider connotations of the term 'performance'. However, since most session musicians do usually seek a public venue at which members of the general public will be present this in itself should be understood as a 'statement'. In a sense the audience is there not to be there. Sessions normally occur among people who know each other, at least to some degree. Although held in a public place, they are not open to general participation. When this does occur it can cause resentment because the presence of a large number of newcomers who have not internalised the appropriate norms of session behaviour can change the nature of the session:

> C: The ... thing you tend to get that can ruin sessions is when they become something popular such as when they are publicised on the local radio station, whereas previously it had been just a few friends and they might invite friends along or other people would turn up to join in or so on, but if it is popularised on local radio you can get groups of people coming along and bringing bodhrans [a type of drum]. [*Laughs*] And I mean a lot of bodhran playing is very very bad. People think that they've just got to hit the thing and it doesn't really matter but bodhrans, because they are a very bassy instruments, can give off a lot of volume and they can really make it more difficult for other musicians to sort of gel and hear each other properly. You come along with a bodhran and you bash it away and very few of these people have any sort of sense of rhythm at all ...

Informality and spontaneity are greatly revered in folk music, but there is a widely held expectation that 'good' music, that is to say, music which is deemed to be every bit as good as music performed on stage, can be heard at sessions. In fact, this frequently goes further and for many people a good session is where the best of folk music is sung and played. Hearing the best of folk music at an event which is itself 'spontaneous' is regarded as a highlight, where the music can be heard at its best in terms of the linking of the music to its setting and in terms of musical quality, though that is not to say that such events necessarily occur often. However, it is in such informal settings as opposed to staged performances that many practitioners believe that the 'real' music is able to reach its heights.

If a folk festival publicises a session on the festival programme this creates a degree of inherent contradiction. An event that is on the programme cannot be spontaneous, but there are reasons why organisers wish to highlight sessions. If these are regarded as high spots of the music, then it is good advertising practice if they are on the programme. The inclusion of sessions and singarounds in publicity allows non-musicians to feel welcome to participate in the informal aspects of the festival. However, when sessions are placed on the programme this is no guarantee that anyone will turn up, and I am aware of many occasions when advertised sessions simply did not happen. Most sessions are not programmed events. Indeed, festival organisers expect this and many state this as a feature of their festivals – that plenty of good informal music can be found. As one folk festival organiser explained to me:

> G: The formality part of the concert is fine for that situation. But the music flourishes because people know that they are in a particular event, they are either in a concert situation, in which case they perform in a certain sort of way but very often the virtuoso parts come out because you've got four whistle players together at 4 o'clock in the morning. Therefore, socially that's the kind of experience, if you're aware of what's going on round about you, that really makes the festival. And even organisers, or organisers more than most who know what's likely to happen, are going to enjoy that best.

Most session musicians expect to be able to play at a folk festival and generally this is welcomed. However, sometimes the presence of sessions at festivals can cause tension on the part of organisers since sessions provide free entertainment and hence detract from the formal events for which an entrance fee has to be paid.

A central feature of a session is its informality. For a good session to occur, one where singers and musicians are able to gather together in some public place, for them to be heard, for the session not to be disrupted by differences of musical direction or any form of external disruption, it is clear that there must be ways of 'staging' it.

Because folk music celebrates a 'front' of informality masking complex rule-governed behaviour, those unfamiliar with sessions can easily misread this type of musical event as an 'anything goes' happening, and cause the session to be disrupted and break down. There are criteria which are generally recognised by session participants as making for a good session. Certain formal features dispose towards session continuity which, when achieved, may cause a session to last for a long time – many hours in some cases.

In Aberdeen I was party to much talk about a session that was to be held at a nearby weekend folk festival at the start of the festival – to get the festival going, so to speak. This was a small festival with no more than one official event on at a time. The session was on the Friday night, to be followed later by a dance. It was arranged in the sense that it was on the programme and it was one of those occasions where the organisers had fixed up with a number of musicians to be there to play music 'spontaneously' and to make sure that there was enough of a nucleus of musicians to ensure that it got going.

But the session broke down totally. The organisers made the mistake of holding it in the room where the dance was to be held and the dance band, needing to set up their equipment and sound system and carry out a sound check, left little time for the session to get going. After playing for an hour the sessioners were very annoyed to be told to stop in order for the dance to start. An hour was considered not long enough for a session and they resented this. When I spoke to the organisers about this it transpired that this was no mistake – they had only intended the session to last for an hour to warm up the dance. Session musicians do not regard themselves as warm-up musicians and if called upon to play in this role expect their services to be appreciated. Most especially, they do not expect to be switched on and off according to an organiser's whim, a feature derived from the structuring of the session itself. It is the ambivalence of the session as performance that helps to create a confusion on the part of non-regular session goers as to the nature of a session.

That a session is far from informal or unstructured is a view held by many of the session musicians I talked to. Most had a clear view of how a session was to be constructed, and what was, and what was not, suitable session behaviour. However, because of the appearance of informality it is easy for rule-breaking to occur, even by musicians, and it takes time for less experienced musicians to acquire good session etiquette. It is when different assumptions are held as to what is appropriate behaviour that the nature of the rules underlying social behaviour is laid bare. Session musicians pay a lot of attention to session etiquette – perhaps because the session is such an ambivalent form of performance. They commonly discuss among themselves whether a session was good, and if not, what went wrong. The following comments from one of my informants, herself an experienced session musician, illustrate aspects of session etiquette and appropriate session behaviour.

R: The problem occurs when you get someone... who can play quite well who has got a specific set of tunes that they want to play no matter what. Sometimes you get someone like Mike who will introduce a set of tunes to a session and people will say, 'Oh those are really amazing – where did you get them?', and then he will play them again and then someone will have got them taped... and then they will start playing them. That works quite well, but he is not looking to dominate the session – it just so happens he has got a set of tunes that he thinks are really good.

That is very different from the sort of person who comes along and is tense about their playing. Often they play too fast and there is no time or space for anyone else to join in and for it to be a communal thing and sometimes if they are very good players and they have got that sort of attitude as well then they ruin the session for other people; they play all the time. Johnny Marnoch's an extreme case in point. It is almost impossible for anyone to play along with him.

NLM: What does he do?

R: The physical thing that he does is interesting. He very often stands up. This is usually bad form in a session unless there is no space and you are standing on the edge. But he very often comes right into the middle of the group and stands up over everybody else and performs to people outside the playing group. That's very odd. Usually you are all sitting all together in a pub round a table, or in a room where you [are] able to hear each other. You have to also have some sort of eye contact. Near enough that you can have a wee chat in between tunes.

Johnny doesn't go through any of that. He very often borrows a fiddle off someone. He used to come in, borrow someone's fiddle and not give it back, stand up making huge sweeping motions with his hand, tune the fiddle or make as if he was tuning the fiddle very very loudly with double-stoppings [playing two strings at once] as if he is signalling 'I am about to perform'.

Because he does that when he performs, he fiddles with the music, he plays runs all the way up the fiddle and then he will launch into something that probably one or two people in the group would be able to play, but he launches into it very fast, very over the top and adds in a bit of 'Paganini'. He is an extreme case.

A really good fiddle player like Mike won't overstep the timing of the playing of the solo. A good session player will do a solo – a complex tune – but they won't then go on and do another one.

It is generally considered that sessions should not be hogged by any one individual. Although this does happen from time to time, when it does, as in the example above, it is greatly resented. This is in itself a characteristic aspect of the folk scene – suppressing overt displays of status and resisting the star syndrome. I was present at one folk festival where singarounds had been placed on the programme.

Folk festival singarounds are structured in a particular way. There is high respect for the person singing, silence in the room (unlike an instrumental session) and resistance to hijacking or hogging by individuals. There is a pattern for turn-taking, normally singers taking turns in order around the room. Turn-taking is usually rigidly adhered to regardless of who is present, thus leaving little room for status hierarchies to evolve, either as a result of any privileged ordering of performance or from an individual's being able to perform for a longer time. However, festival guests are often put in charge of a session, to act loosely as an MC and ensure continuity. At this festival a singer, one of the famous 'names' of the folk scene, sang six songs in a row at a formally programmed session. This was frowned upon. The function of a star who is appointed to mind a session is to sit there and listen to the contributions of others and partake to no lesser or greater degree.

At instrumental sessions there is also a general expectation of performance. The aim is to perform rather than listen to any particular higher-status performer, but in an instrumental session, unlike most singing sessions, every musician joins in for most of the time. As one session musician put it:

The length of time you don't play is very crucial. If you don't get to play at least one tune in however many, it's going to be a bad session for you . . .

I like the idea that you have a group sound. The idea that you participate with other people to make a sound together. But sometimes I have this aggressive feeling that I must get some playing in . . .

Although it is frowned on for one player to 'hog' a session, there can also be a problem if too many players are reticent and not instigating tunes. At one particular session I had been keeping a 'back seat'. After a time I suspected that this was making some of the musicians uncomfortable and they started encouraging me to instigate a tune. An important factor in a session is its momentum, and some sessions last as long as six hours. For this to occur a certain tension has to be produced. This depends not only on suitability of the performing arena – enough seats, the right level of noise and so on – but also on keeping going, ensuring that there are not too many breaks between tunes, and that there is a reciprocity of turn-taking in instigating tunes. Although I was joining in the tunes by playing the fiddle, my failure to instigate tunes was a threat to session continuity and momentum, and after a while I began to detect an uneasiness. I should add that it took me nearly two hours to realise this was due to my own behaviour! My discreet manner was in fact inadvertently breaking the mores of the event.

A good session will normally last for a considerable time with a minimum of people joining or leaving. Certain devices can be employed to facilitate this continuity. I went to one after-hours session at which a 'wink-man', as I came to call him, emerged. He was not appointed. Everyone was having a good time and wanted the session to continue, but given the early hour of the morning, we would probably have been thrown out of the bar if we had wanted to stay solely for drink. The 'wink-man' would wink at someone during the preceding musical item to indicate that they should perform next and ensured there was always someone ready to give the next song or tune without a lull, and the session ran on this formula from midnight to 4.00 a.m. – a successful attempt to prevent the natural cycle of a session with its high spots and lulls.

Thus the construction of informality so important to most folk scene performances becomes the defining criterion of the session and the singaround.

11   Sources of Status

Within a dominant ideology which emphasises the celebration of participation and informality, status remains. Many folk performers stake a claim to distinction based upon their familiarity with traditional music. Thus within the folk scene there is a great status to be gained from finding a 'new' folk song. If the song is not generally known in revival circles considerable kudos can attach to finding such a 'new' old song. The high status afforded to originality of material but not original material is a striking paradox of the genre. One of the audience questionnaire respondents mentioned as a pet hate 'those who seek their material from the latest Martin Carthy record', Martin Carthy being probably the most famous of modern revival singers. Many respondents mentioned that copying repertoire from records of revival performers was something they particularly frowned upon. Established performers do sing and play material used by other people as long as it is not too closely associated with that performer. However, to be taken at all seriously, 'making a song one's own' is an essential requirement; and this means being taken seriously by those that matter, chiefly those who control access to events – festival and club booking secretaries.

Anyone wanting a paid gig or trying to build up a reputation as a 'revivalist' has to place an individual 'stamp' on material which can become identified as 'theirs', often by finding one of the 'new' old songs or through a process of straightforward musical appropriation whereby a song, while known to some degree, is performed with the adoption of stylistic changes. This might include the addition of a virtuoso instrumental arrangement, so that this song becomes especially associated with that singer.

An example of a song which, although not hitherto well known in the folk scene, was easily accessible from song collections, is Martin Carthy's arrangement of 'Famous Flower of Serving Men'. His virtuosic guitar accompaniment and its highly melodic relationship to the vocals give this song a 'stamp' which closely identifies it with him. He is frequently asked to perform this song and the technical sophistication of the accompaniment and the fact that this accompaniment is so stylised renders the song, for the time being at least, outwith the general source repertoire of traditional material for upwardly aspiring revival folk singers. Thus the song has been to all intents and purposes appropriated by him.

This appropriation of traditional material is by no means peculiar to the folk scene. Ginette Dunn (1980), writing about the singing traditions of East Suffolk and specifically about the group of singers who frequent a pub called the Blaxhall Ship, mentions that most of the singers had an idea that certain songs belong to certain singers. This also applied to songs that were known not to be specific to Blaxhall and which were therefore contained in the repertoire of other singers outwith the village. But within the village a certain degree of song ownership was evidenced. As one of her informants remarked:

> Your own song, they called for you, you go into the Ship, I heard 'em say, you go into the Ship, and they call a song from so-and-so and they had their one song to sing and that was that, weren't it? And if they sung anyone else's that was warfare straight away.
>
> (Dunn 1980: 189)

One of my respondents was most forthright on this. She was a Scottish fiddle player who had had a long experience of playing in sessions and had also played in various semi-professional folk bands:

> People have these ideas about tunes belonging to themselves. You internalise a tune, you make it your own, you perform it, it's associated with you . . . It has these two aspects. One that you internalise the tune and learn it yourself and have the style yourself – you play it your way. The second thing is that it is part of a common repertoire. This paradox becomes more marked when you then add on the extra thing of being a professional performer, because then something manifests itself which is that people say things to you like, 'Oh we can't play that tune because such and such has recorded it; we can't do that one because that's so and so's tune'. For instance I play a tune called 'The Sound of Sleat'. Now I can't remember how I learned it – I don't have any Ossian albums as it happens, but I have since discovered it is on an Ossian album which is now used as a theme tune for a radio programme. I just played it because I picked it up from – wherever. In a way it's a naff tune as a result. It has this label because it's been played by these other people. That is a tune that would never be performed by the band I play in because it has these connotations, though we play it in sessions etc. So that's an example of a tune having this dual thing that it belongs to somebody and yet it's part of the common repertoire.

The notion of the 'common repertoire' is central to the folk scene as a genre, and it is scarcely surprising that this should create tensions for musicians who are setting out to establish their own status and individuality. In the light of such factors as a desire to prove one's self as a musician or to gain respect from one's peers, we can see how tensions can be generated from within a prevailing ethos that suppresses overt attention to self. But how is the central ethos pertaining to the notion of communality of music in the folk scene maintained, by whom and for what reasons; and how are attempts made to subvert this?

It is the ambivalence of repertoire continuity – that songs are part of a common tradition – that has set up this conflict. Since a folk performer today is exposed to the role models of performers in other musical genres, we should not be surprised that these may 'contaminate' the values of the folk scene. For instance, the cult of individualism and personality that surrounds rock superstars may also be cultivated by successful folk performers.

However this would an over-simplification. It is not the case that the tradition was originally somehow 'purer' and isolated from such tendencies because, as Dunn indicates, this duality between a song as belonging to somebody and yet being part of a common repertoire was recognised by the singers in the Blaxhall Ship. These traditional or source singers are possessive with regard to repertoire. Dunn mentions how there is an understanding that a singer's repertoire will not usurped by others, especially if that person's repertoire is small. But on the other hand the singers were conscious of the importance of the need for transmission:

> G.D.: Would the old singers mind if one of the young ones picked up one of theirs?
> A.L.: Oh, no, no. Oooh, a lot of them used to learn them, that's how Cyril came to get a lot of my father's. He learn them off him, and Father didn't mind (Dunn 1980: 189).

But others did mind, though they might also be chastised for this possessiveness:

> G.D.: Do you know 'Underneath the Apron'?
> P.W.: I can sing it but that's Bob Hart's song.
> G.D.: Will you sing it?
> P.W.: Yer, I'll sing it. [*Sings*]
> G.D.: Where did you learn it?
> P.W.: Oh I learnt it down there. [Butley Oyster]
> G.D.: Who from?
> P.W.: Well, they say that was Bob Hart. But a mate, Peter Benstead, he learnt that off Bob Hart, and Bob said, 'Don't sing my song' . . . 'cos he thinks I'm giving his songs away. Well, I told him then, they weren't his songs. They were sung to him from other people, 'cos a lot of Blaxhall old people learnt him a lot of those songs, yer (Dunn 1980: 191).

From the comments of my and Dunn's informants, we can see that the folk revival and the folk tradition have many facets in common with regard to ownership of repertoire. This is because a central function of the relationship of the musicians/singers to the common body of repertoire has remained the same. The revival has retained this notion of a corpus of commonly owned material which can be considered as 'on loan' to certain individuals at given moments. But as we can see from Dunn's interviews, a common repertoire did not mean a form of musical communality. The status of individual performers became intimately bound up with the performance of 'their' songs. If it was 'his' or 'her' song a singer could still be heard with respect even if it was the only song he or she knew. In these circumstances it was especially frowned upon to 'poach' such a song (Dunn 1980: 196).

My informant above recognises that control over repertoire is important with regard to attributes of status:

I have this thing about dance repertoire as distinct from session repertoire and normal performance repertoire. I think that people do that quite often. They have a tune, but they won't perform it in a session if it is a tune that they like performing. I have a certain reluctance to play certain sets of tunes. I have four tunes which I learned from an old guy in Edinburgh and I have a reluctance to teach them to anyone else. In my mind I don't want them to learn it. People do play them. It's just that when people say, 'play a tune', and it's a formal situation – a folk club or a ceilidh, I want to have a tune that I can play that people aren't going to know. I suppose it's that I don't want other performers to say, 'Oh, not that tune, I can play that'.

In this case she is concerned that her identification with these tunes would cease if they became more widely known, and, as she specifically mentions, she wants some of her repertoire to be unfamiliar to her audience. Either way it is evident that there are factors of status at work here and that this musician feels that, to a certain degree, she has special claim on some of the material she plays, even though she may have learned it from other people.

Song and tune appropriation can function as claims to distinction. 'Ladders' or pecking orders become apparent among folk musicians because some individuals are more able to appropriate material than others, that is to say, their claims to distinction will be more readily accepted. In the example above, my informant considered herself threatened and therefore must view herself as located some way down the scale of the status hierarchy.

In the folk scene gambits are also forwarded with regard to certain stylistic effects in performance. Some well-known and respected singers and musicians have adopted certain stylistic effects which have become their own personal markers. This might not seem to be remarkable in the context of musical genres generally, but it is certainly paradoxical when we consider that many of these singers were trying to revive a 'traditional' form of singing style. In fact the status games played over the stylistic effects came to inhibit the adoption of such effects by other musicians, even though they were in origin drawn from the folk tradition. One such musical feature is the exaggerated 'sliding' onto notes adopted by Martin Carthy. Although based on traditional singing styles, the fact that he was chiefly responsible for introducing this effect into the folk revival has rendered it inaccessible since he has to some extent 'appropriated' it.

Again this discussion crosses the divide into those realms of musical performance which relate to attempts by musicians to affirm their own individuality and status as musicians. This has profound effects upon the direction of the folk scene as a genre. It is not simply a case of singers wishing to re-create or rediscover traditional singing styles, since the dynamics of interpersonal interaction with regard to these musical gambits distort this possibility. The role played by gambits for distinction serves as a barrier to the transmission of idiom. Underlying this is the existence of a musical hierarchy in the folk scene, albeit within a prevailing ideology which downplays it. In one sense the prevailing ideology ensures that claims to distinction have to be made more covertly than they would in other musical genres. Audiences screaming their adulation, or reaching out to touch an artist, and the jet set/hotel/fast car type of distancing is 'out', and thus what is 'in', what performers seek to make distinct about themselves, has to be rendered more discreet.

The seriousness and air of veneration which surrounds the musical repertoire leads a status game to be fought out over the actual musical repertoire itself – who sings and plays what and how they do it.

Another well-known and respected folk revival singer has made blatant bids for a highly individualistic style of song presentation. First and foremost, this is evidenced in his musical style. He has accentuated a form of 'guttural rumbling' in his vocal treatment of songs, again like Martin Carthy's sliding stylistic effect, that is found among 'source' singers from the folk tradition, though he has greatly accentuated this. Although a singer of collected 'source' songs, he performs in very 'zany' clothes – orange, open-breasted T-shirts, earrings, hair dyed in primary colours and a small pigtail. This was thought extreme and was much remarked upon. He came to be regarded as a carica-ture of himself, a caricature which in 'glam rock' might be acceptable, essential even, but in the folk scene it led to his popularity waning for a while. The folk scene tends to shrink from overtly stylised presentations of self. An underlying seriousness permeates the genre and does not permit the sort of 'send-up' which characterises 'glam rock' performances.

Jokes, 'crack', and so on are present in the folk scene, as is parody, a theme already touched on, but a strong and serious commitment to the musical content dominates. This particularly applies to the way the music might be seen by outsiders. To give another example, the local independent televi-sion station for my area occasionally features folk music on its tea-time magazine programme. Musicians from Aberdeen folk club are sometimes asked to appear. A continual gripe from the musicians is the way the television company tries to trivialise folk music. Many producers, unfamiliar with folk music, regard it with a quaint, 'yokel' air. One local band in Aberdeen was asked to play on the programme and was provided with a hay cart to sit on, and, being surprised and 'put on the spot', grudgingly agreed to perform on it. When the programme went out on the air scorn was heaped on them by their fellow folk musicians for having done this. Tich Frier remarked:

> *T*: Generally [in the media] they are very nice people. They just never listen. They've just got no conception that . . . they've established this format for what folk shows should be like nearly thirty years ago and that's it. They've got their ideas about what a folk singer looks like. They do not wear suits. [He tried to wear a suit in one programme and they would not let him.]
>
> *NLM*: Do they try and restrict what you actually do, or make you sit on straw bales?
>
> *T*: Oh aye! Sitting on straw bales is a favourite. They've always got you sitting on straw bales.

Within folk circles the music itself is venerated. Joking and a light-hearted form of presentation are welcomed, but within this framework there is a shared understanding of underlying seriousness. When a performer's jokes draw so much attention that the centrality of the music is threatened, this can be seen as stepping over a boundary. This seriousness of presentation is often used as a marker of distinction and status. Thus a static, dour presentation of a song, what is often referred to in the folk scene as a 'finger-in-the-ear style', could in itself be a powerful claim to distinction, one which demonstrates a serious commitment. This serious approach is in evidence at many song 'workshops' – a sort of academic paper-cum-musical performance particularly common at folk festivals.

Many respondents picked up on this snobbishness attaching to repertoire selection. A wide repertoire drawing upon a corpus of traditional material and a deep knowledge of the historical contexts of a song are greatly respected. It is not enough to have sufficient repertoire to fill a performance spot or even the performing spots of a whole folk festival. Someone like Martin Carthy is respected not just for his performances in isolation, but because of his vast repertoire and knowledge of Britain's folk music traditions.

This has not only put him at the top of the status league of British revival folk singers, it also keeps him there. A claim to distinction on this criterion is highly sustainable. While a very high level of performing ability can be attained by the musically talented relatively readily (in a few years), the demonstration of such a depth of knowledge of this traditional corpus of material and its historical connections takes decades. Therefore a far more subtle process may be operating with regard to the folk scene's maintenance of historical continuity as a dominant element in its socio-musical ideology, a process which works against the non-hierarchical, accessible 'do-it-yourself' ethos that manifests itself as dominant on the surface.

Control over musical repertoire can inform us not only about the underlying musical ideology of the folk scene but also about how this functions to maintain the folk scene as a social system. Whereas in many musical genres it is performing ability or the creation of a star syndrome which forms a key component of distancing, the folk scene places further layers of inaccessibility on this. Thus to interpret surface features of the organisation of the musical event in the folk scene as mere suppression of hierarchy is a gross over-simplification. It is very difficult for a new star to burst upon the folk scene and it is difficult for those in the highest-status roles as performers on the folk scene to be treated as superstars. The relationship between the folk scene and the folk tradition in fact makes it possible for those with sufficient depth of knowledge to be placed in high-status roles and to stay there for long periods of time.

Martin Carthy has been the foremost touring folk singer of the revival for nearly thirty years. Although little known outwith the folk scene his reputation within it is paramount. This is in itself an oddity. A partial explanation is that Carthy's high-status rests so much on a criterion that could not be understood from outwith the genre – his deep knowledge of Britain's traditional song heritage. In most music scenes the foremost performers come to have a reputation outside. The fact that this is generally not the case for the folk scene in itself indicates that the folk scene does not present its successes in the manner of other contemporary musical genres. We can begin to see deeper significance in the articulation of a concept such as 'tradition'. As a device which sustains performers in a high-status position, and keeps them there, it has a powerful ideological function. It has become a status marker.

We must be aware that claims to distinction and markers of distinction are not just given *per se*. They are gambits, and, as in the opening gambit of a game of chess, they can be accepted or declined. Because one marker becomes dominant this must not be allowed to mask the fact that a host of competing gambits or claims to distinction are made but only some are 'admitted'. To add a further complication, such gambits may be accepted by one group and rejected by another and it is from this differential acceptance that musical sub-genres emerge. The folk scene as a genre contains sub-groups whose ideology is different in certain respects. It is here that the problem of boundaries creeps in. When a gambit for distinction is made but accepted by only certain groups of people, it is difficult to discern whether such a group is now to be considered as outwith the genre or comprising merely a sub-group of it. In some ways this is purely academic, but in other ways it essentially affects the coherence of the genre.

Certainly many other performing ethics than those which dominate in British folk clubs have been applied to the corpus of traditional folk song. The songs have been sung in farm bothies, arranged by classical composers such as Benjamin Britten and sung in classical style by Peter Pears in a concert hall setting, and have been performed by various more popularly orientated performers from the Pogues to the Corries. The above are outwith the modern folk scene if only because they do not perform within it, although it is important to note that folk songs are sung outwith the folk scene and that the present-day organisation of the folk scene and its dominant socio-musical ideology is not configured in the musical form itself, though it has borrowed certain paramusical features from the folk tradition.

Apart from performing or singing, another way to establish closeness with key performers is to be an organiser. This became apparent in arranging one interview for this study. The singer was playing at the local university folk club near where I live, and we had arranged the interview while he was in town. Since he had to get back home early the next day he suggested that we conduct the interview directly after the gig. I thought it would make sense for me to accommodate him for the night but he was concerned about this. He was concerned about offending the organisers and mentioned that he had discovered how, for many organisers, 'putting up' the guest was considered a perk of the job.

At many folk festivals this familiarity with the guests is openly flaunted, though it is true that the custom of staying in organisers' houses means that the promoters, organisers and performers are often on very good terms and are in most cases genuinely good friends. But this social mixing serves the function of allowing people whose musical and performing abilities would not permit them to climb the performing ladder to mix with performers. The ethos of participation permits this mixing but also creates a hierarchy of events, one which can utilise informality in an unofficial reversal of the significance of those events which are 'officially' the most important.

At most folk festivals it is at the official programmed events that there is the greatest tendency towards a performer–audience relationship in the conventional sense. Many of the musicians I spoke to saw this as the most 'worklike' part of playing at festivals. It is after official gigs at the after-hours events that musicians let their hair down and the 'real' crack can occur. But not all those who attend folk festivals are aware of or have access to after-hours crack. Being 'in the know' attributes to itself high kudos. A status game ensues where the official events are treated with disdain. This disdain reinforces the fact that one is getting crack elsewhere and, in consequence, even these 'informal' events can become formalised. At one folk festival there was a hotel for the 'real' guests only – and this was exclusive.

At another Scottish folk festival I noticed that there was an after-hours event but that this was regulated by ticket access. The idea was that it was a place for performers and friends to have a few drinks and wind down after official performances, to be followed by a relaxed music session. This was how it was described to me, though it was far from how it turned out. First, the allocation of tickets engendered exclusivity. The event became widely known and many festival goers tried to but could not get in. At another festival which had a similar after-hours event the exclusivity was such that even many noted performers could not get in, which caused much bad feeling, not just because they felt excluded by friends, but also because late at night there was literally nowhere else to go and have a session. At Keith Festival one such after-hours session has even become ritualised in a very odd way. Sheer pressure of numbers meant that not everyone could get into after-hours events, official or unofficial, and the singing session at 2.00 a.m. in the festival camp toilets has become a feature of the festival. At another folk festival the official after-hours session was much talked about. Guests and non-guests who were not booked but who were of a high status would do 'spots'. This event came to be the place where these guests would be in a situation of singing to their peers. It became the venue where performers would try to be at their best, to sing or play the best of their repertoire, yet it had the trappings of informality and spontaneity; there was no stage and people would perform from different positions around the room. Despite the trappings of informality which marked a performance spot the audience was composed of fellow performers, and forgetting words or a bad performance here could mean much more to a performer than at an official event.

Another marker of status is 'being known'. I noticed this myself when I turned up to a folk club on an open night, that is, a night where there is no guest performer. The organisers knew me as a musician, though it was not a club that I had regularly attended. During the performance the MC made reference to me in a joking fashion, and I was asked to finish the night's performance. In another instance I became aware of the offence that this can arouse for some performers precisely when such attention is not given. The

Saturday afternoon concert at weekend festivals is normally a 'come all ye' and features less of the booked guests of the festival and plenty of floor spots. This is the time when musicians who have just turned up to the festival and who are not booked can perform. Occasionally, as a mark of respect, such a person or group might be put on in an official evening concert despite not having been booked for the festival. But on one particular occasion a singer who turned up to a Saturday afternoon concert was not invited to perform while another well-known singer of similar standing who was not booked for that festival was put on. Afterwards she 'cornered' the organisers to express her annoyance – to their astonishment, I might add. They had seen this as giving her a break from singing, but the singer took it as a snub. Again status games are in full view here.

At this festival those wishing to perform indicated their willingness to the MC. This singer, being well known, did not feel she had to do this and I am sure that this was taken by the organisers as meaning that she did not wish to perform. In this way the signals are ambivalent. Those seeking status do not wish to be seen to be asking for its overt demonstration, but there are strategies which are adopted to facilitate status enhancement.

A similar occurrence was described to me by another (semi-professional) performer who, because she had recently been the booked guest at the folk club, expected that she would be able to get free entry in return for playing a floor spot:

> Having to pay to get in to play that was the kiss of death for folk clubs as far as I was concerned. . . . The killer came when I turned up to see somebody I wanted to see at a folk club and had an instrument with me and was prepared to do a floor spot and they told me I had to pay to get in as well. That was absolute death as far as I was concerned.

This sort of attitude arouses strong feelings within the folk scene. However, it does provide evidence of an audience–performer differentiation. This performer's status as a musician, as one who performs in a band that had been booked at this club, indicated to her that she should perform as a floor performer and not be expected to pay. Having been a guest at the club and then been expected to pay was an insult, an assault on her 'front' (Goffman 1963). At many folk clubs an air of aloofness is generated by attenders' not sitting down even when there are seats available – staying at the back of the room, propping up the bar and so on. By doing this, these people give off an air of withdrawal, of not looking keen. Often I noticed that this was so striking as to cause a gaping hole of seats at the front of the room while at the back people were standing crammed together. At one club I was told that the club was always like this, and it was always the same people, those who were most closely associated with organising and running the club, who were crammed at the bar. Performers would sometimes make a joke out of the fact that there were rows of empty seats at the front.

Within folk music there is a diversity of stances relating to musical ideology. Some elements of this diversity might appear in conflict with the dominant ethos of the folk scene and may even act as focuses for possible changes in the overall socio-musical framework. But it is not always appropriate to discount counter-instances as exceptions, as if they were some form of socio-musical 'contamination'. If a certain socio-musical configuration is to remain dominant within a genre then the counter-instances must, at least to some degree, be seen as integral to the genre. I am pointing to a conceptualisation of socio-musical ideology as process. It is never static. It dynamically derives from the interplay of social interaction within the genre. An ideal typification hides a more complicated constellation of values and practices. Many of these are in opposition to the dominant socio-musical ideology which in consequence has to be restated and reaffirmed.

A superficial interpretation of performance in the folk scene as the celebration of convivial values would miss how informality itself functions as a marker of distinction. The informality is a key element which can itself produce hierarchy – and at many folk festivals this has been ritualised. But what remains dominant in the organising ethic or socio-musical ideology is not static. Where it is, or seems to be so, it is because elements of that ideology serve individuals' purposes. As the needs of individuals alter, so might the prevailing dominant ideology, and it is from this dynamic perspective that changes in the socio-musical aesthetic should be examined. For instance, the lessening of the importance of traditional songs in the folk scene today might be a result of the difficulty on the part of newer singers to unearth many more 'new' old songs and could also be interpreted as a challenge to the ethos of 'depth of knowledge' as a requirement for high respect. It could therefore be a challenge to the sustainability of this requirement and interpreted as a challenge by newer singers to the dominant generation of folk revivalists who have built an ideology which successfully sustains themselves in a high-status position within the genre. It might have nothing to do with changing relationships to the past and to 'tradition' as an organising concept in itself.

The socio-musicological ideology of the folk scene as a genre, and by extension that of any musical genre, only exists at any given juncture as a resultant of many given differential pressures for change. Those which dominate at any given point could be said to typify the genre. But herein lies the danger of using ideal types as a method for investigation. If what is deemed legitimate as opposed to deviant at any given time among specific groups of people in a musical genre is in a state of flux, with a dominant ethos having to be continually reaffirmed in competition with alternative ideologies, this presents a danger as to the selection of the typifications and ideal types which 'represent' the genre. Those features which could be viewed as 'subversive' to the prevailing ethos of the genre may be as important, and it might even be the case that a given ethos only remains dominant because competing pressures from differing subverting ideologies cancel each other out.

For this reason the study of the exceptional, the micro or the search for seemingly trivial clues in seeking to identify why a given aspect of a dominant ideology remains dominant may be as valid as the identification and listing of the features of ideal typologies, and in my view provides a more penetrating and explanatory social scientific account. In the folk scene I have indicated that there are certain powerful structuring ideologies, but these are utilised at the individual level in ways which are often at odds with the over-arching ethos. It may even be the case that the dominant ethos is 'permitted' to remain because it provides a 'cover' for the articulation of alternative values which therefore benefit from remaining covert or understated. Certainly informality, spontaneity, continuity and an ethos of participation are dominant features of the folk scene. But they are also organising concepts which are utilised as ideological tools, and they are used by individuals for reasons. The interests of club organisers, floor performers, professional touring performers, agents, record promoters and so on all differ. The way in which musical ideologies are articulated affects the distribution of power. It is this tussle for power – for status, 'recognition', a better fee and so on – that feeds these ideological disputes which in turn, through their articulation, structure the forms of musical performance.

12 *Amplification: A Pointer to the Future?*

Of the innovations spreading through the folk scene, the way in which amplification or 'PA' (from public address system) is employed may be indicative of the general artistic direction in which the folk scene is heading. The use of PA strikes at the core of the staging of events, the nature of the performer–audience relationship and the 'here-and-now' nature of musical presentation.

PA has been used in folk festivals at concerts for a long time with little controversy, mainly because of the size of the venues and frequent lack of good acoustics. However, traditional folk music was not designed for the stage and the means of vocal production it employs do not normally use special techniques to project the voice such as those employed by classically trained singers. Until recently PA has not been widely used in folk clubs.

PA is now used at many folk clubs which had functioned adequately for years without them. Several respondents recognised that this induced changes in the nature of the audience–performer relationship and expressed their sensitivity. Paul Metzers, a professional folk singer, is typical:

NLM: You said you prefer not to use PA. Why?

P: I use it if the organiser has said, 'Yes, we're in a room where you need a PA.' So if I've been told that, I put it up because I feel the organiser knows his club, and he knows better than I do. Sometimes I've turned up and found the organiser has said to use the PA because they like to use the PA, but not because the room needs it. I like to use a PA in a room that needs it because it saves me wearing my voice out. It makes the job a lot easier for me . . .

NLM: You say you prefer not to if the room's right. Why?

P: Because it's something between you and the audience; not so much an obstacle but a barrier. It distances you from the audience, because the sound – and they're always conscious of it that what they are getting is a sound – has been amplified, and it sounds as though it's been amplified. And I suppose gradually as you and the audience get used to it, you can overcome that but it's always a barrier in the first instance, and sometimes it stays there all night – definitely to chorus singing, without exception.

This effect of PA upon chorus singing was mentioned by several respondents. Aberdeen folk club is one of the clubs that has taken to using PA consistently in recent years. Here chorus singing is now of a fairly muted nature but several informants mentioned that the club was at one time renowned for its chorus singing.

Another of the clubs that I concentrated upon, the Hoy at Anchor folk club in Essex, is one of those that still does not normally use PA, expressly because of its deleterious effect upon the willingness of audiences to join in with choruses. It is, however, occasionally used in this club, but for a special reason, as explained by Bryan Martin, the club's chairman:

> Some people say 'Right – no amplification', but that's a bit silly because there's a lot of groups these days who use really odd combinations of instruments which nevertheless sound great but only when they are properly balanced. But Battlefield [a folk band] using the war-pipes without amplification – that's all you're going to hear; only for balance, you certainly don't need amplification for anything else in a room like that. The acoustics are quite good. You don't need volume. Clannad brought a whole load of amplification gear but the volume was at an acoustic level . . . It was obviously superb amplification gear and they purely used it to balance the voices and the instruments. Their sound man is a genius . . . it was almost no louder than an unamplified group.

However, PA is becoming much more commonly used by performers. Alan Taylor, a touring semi-professional folk club singer, explains why he now almost always uses it:

> The dynamic range on an acoustic gig can't always be as wide as it can be on a PA gig. For example, if you are using a PA, the dynamic range between whispering and full volume is quite wide. Now if it is an acoustic gig you can't whisper at that volume because no one would hear it, so the dynamic range has gone smaller. Your whisper can't be a real whisper, it must be a stage whisper. So you lose a lot of the softer end of the bottom range because it just won't penetrate. So you can't get the breadth of emotion.
>
> On an acoustic gig your volume is starting at a higher level. On a scale from 1 to 10 it might be starting from a level of 3 or 4, but with a PA you can start right down at 1. The second point which can sometimes be a hindrance is that you will hear your voice coming back to you from the PA. You tend to judge the tone of your voice by what you're hearing through the PA. When you're acoustic you have to get used to listening to your own voice in your ear again and adjusting your tone.
>
> I work with the volume set at such a level that I like to think of it as amplified acoustic sound as opposed to electronic sound. So I usually work my PA in such a way that I can hear them coming back. But I find I do a better performance in a club the size of last night with a good PA because it makes me feel good and the better I feel the more I enjoy my sound the better I'm going to perform.

PA is being used in the folk scene but in a specialised way which has been adapted to the ethos of the scene. Alan Taylor uses PA to enable the employment of a greater dynamic range in venues whose acoustics is not commensurate with their size. But he stands at a crossroads in terms of the presentational ethos of the folk scene, and the changing role of PA is at the centre of this. PA does not just raise the volume level but also redefines the nature of the performance, and is itself a powerful statement of the separation of roles of performer and audience. It restructures the power relationship. It becomes difficult for audiences to sing choruses because of the greater volume of the performer and it prevents heckles and interjections by the audience for the same reason.

Because an acoustic performance can be so easily marred by intrusions of extraneous noise, from a general bustle at the bar to background chatter, this imposes a constraint upon a folk audience, one which is integral to the structuring of the musical event. Once the possibility of disruption has been lessened by the use of PA, it is not simply the case that audibility is greater – the likelihood that any disruption could affect the performance is now much lower. No longer is it the case that anyone who talks through a performance will disrupt that very performance. A general rise in level of background talking is widely reported throughout the folk scene following the advent of PA. However, this point arouses much controversy.

I attended the annual general meeting of a club which had recently come to use PA at virtually every folk club night, whereas until only a few years previously it had used it only occasionally. Two main viewpoints split the room evenly. The first claimed that with the advent of the use of PA there was now much background talking at the bar. There was no longer an intensity associated with listening to performers. The general informality of the club, which all recognised and saw as a distinctive feature of the club, had now shifted towards a general disrespect towards performers. They claimed that there was a trend away from participation towards a general atmosphere which was discouraging floor singers.

The pro-PA camp claimed that to ignore and discourage PA was to fail to move with the times and that this was a fault of the folk scene which was discouraging younger people from entering the scene. It was claimed that a 'sanctimonious hush' gave an overly serious tone to the proceedings and a small amount of background noise was welcomed. Use of PA gave the performer greater musical control over their performance and favoured singers who had less powerful voices. A suggestion made by this group was that if some people objected to the use of PA they were quite at liberty not to use it but that the PA should always be set up in any case for those who wanted to use it.

This also raised strong feelings. The 'anti' camp claimed that if one person used PA the volume level was set for that night and disposed towards background chatter. Then, when someone followed playing acoustically, the lowering of dynamics made that person sound flat. The 'antis' claimed that the PA equipment was in itself inadequate. For instance, on many occasions in this club, microphones of an incompatible impedance to the amplifier had been used, there was no mixing of sound during the performance, and broken microphone stands which could not be adjusted for the singer's height had been used. The equipment would often emit a gentle 'hum'.

While some of the 'antis' pointed this out in discussion it appeared that many of the 'pros' were not aware of this, or else it did not seem to bother them to anything like the same degree. It was the 'antis' who seemed particularly concerned that there was 'a PA sound' that was distinct from acoustic sound.

In addition, points were made by the 'antis' that few people in the club were experienced in the vocal techniques necessary for the proper use of PA. Freedom of movement in performance would be constricted in order to remain within the dynamic range of the microphones. Finally, the system was normally only set up and balanced for the guest performer, who would sound-check prior to the start of the evening. This was claimed by the 'antis' to have the effect of making many floor performers seem and sound less accomplished than they really were and set up a more powerful barrier between the guests and those floor performers who were not experienced in using PA. Thus the 'antis' came round to a perhaps surprising argument that if there was to be continued use of PA at the club then this should then be treated much more professionally; the sound should be mixed by an appointed mixing person to be provided with a mixing desk, singers should be trained in how to use PA, and closer attention should be paid to the PA equipment itself.

The upshot of this discussion was that impedance adaptors were bought for the microphones and the broken microphone stand was replaced, but none of the other points raised was implemented. These arguments were revealing with regards to inherent tensions over general artistic direction.

PA is coming to be used more widely throughout the folk clubs. The function of raising volume is only the most basic of sound modifications made possible by the use of electronic equipment. What is most indicative is that for a long time the use of PA has been resisted by the folk scene. Comments on the use of PA were made by many informants, and again I quote Alan Taylor:

NLM: I notice that background noise bothers you.
A: Well I don't see the point of someone coming in, paying money to come and see me or go to a folk club and talking because, apart from the fact that it does distract the rest of the audience – they've paid their money and deserve the right to listen if they want to – I'm not background music. If I was background music, I'd be playing in bars and most probably be earning a lot more money. That's not what I've chosen to do, so unless you meet me half-way and you are prepared to work with me on getting into the lyrics and what the song's about there's very little point listening.

It is the only place in Britain where you will get people working on the lyrics. Most live gigs of pop groups the words are almost unintelligible because of the venue and the amount of PA and the emphasis on the music and rhythm. On an album it's slightly different. If you listen to the Smiths' album, for example, you can hear all the words and they are printed on the sleeve so they are obviously concerned about the lyrics. But if you go to one of their live gigs it would be very difficult to hear what they are singing about ...

I was a bit annoyed about the noise at the bar. And the people who talked three-quarters of the way through 'Roll on the Day'. But that distresses me because I think it's such an important song about such an important issue. How can you have the audacity to talk through it? People's bad manners amaze me.

The conflict of socio-musical ideology cannot be understood without reference to the role of music in wider society. Two important uses of music stand out. One is the restructuring of listening consciousness caused by the ubiquitous presence of recorded music; the other is the blurring of a distinction between live and recorded music in live performance. The potentialities of electronic equipment are such that most music is written and performed not so much for live performance as for recordings. This then has the effect that music becomes ever more difficult to reproduce in live performance. Use of special techniques and backing tapes has become commonplace and live performance has, in many musical genres, become largely secondary in importance to recorded music.

However, it would not be strictly accurate to say that the folk scene exists in direct opposition to this general trend in the evolution of the form of musical performance. The sound potentialities of new technology are being explored in the folk scene, but with limitations. There is no headlong rush into the use of special effects, although they are coming to be used. This slower uptake is almost certainly due to the central role of live performance in the genre. Many folk performers who play in bands frequently return to performing acoustically and informally in some contexts. This is in stark contrast to Bennett's (1980) findings relating to US rock performers.

It is difficult to predict what the outcome of this trend is likely to be. On the one hand the emphasis upon informality, directness, and on unmediated acoustic performance, may be merely acting as a brake upon evolution of the performance aesthetic, which in other musical genres was not hampered by these ideological elements. If this is the case folk music will move in the general direction of the presentational ethic of mainstream popular music. However, on the basis of the evidence so far presented about the nature of staging, the nature of lyrical communication, and the celebration of informality in the folk scene, I am going to suggest that we are more likely to see the introduction of new technological possibilities which are adapted to the existing performance aesthetic rather than for it to cause any fundamental shift of ethos. In other words, changing technological possibilities will not, by themselves, destroy the socio-musical ideology of the folk scene.

For example, the discussion which took place at the folk club AGM mentioned previously was resolved through a generally accepted compromise that, if the folk scene was going to 'move with the times' then the ways in which it should do so – for instance, in introducing PA – should be managed with the utmost care so as not to destroy the essence of the folk club; that the platform offered by the folk clubs was not to be allowed to become a general live music venue; that there was a special type of music performed which could be characterised in the ethos of its performance; the fact that this was a folk club and not some other kind of live-music event.

Chelmsford folk club also offered some interesting indicators on this issue. It is one that has whole-heartedly embraced the use of PA – but in a very specialised way. The club had been following the pattern of the gradual introduction of PA and had just bought its own PA for the first time when I visited. The organisers explained the reason for this to me:

> *S*: The room we're in is a sort of half and half room. Sometimes you need PA and sometimes you don't.
> *NLM*: Why?
> *S*: Just the size of the room. Some people can project their music and some can't... The way we left it in the past was if the guests came along and they wanted to use their PA they were welcome to, but otherwise we ran acoustically.

These club organisers stated that they had been thinking of buying PA equipment for several years but were concerned about the possible of effects of this change. When I visited the club the PA equipment had been installed and in use for only three weeks. On the night a fairly new and popular band, Blowzabella, were the guests. The first thing that was apparent was that no microphones were actually visible. Only the odd wire trailing down the side walls from an area of the stage above the performers gave a clue to the presence of the PA. The microphones in use were pressure-zone microphones which look like two flat plates. Here they were stuck to the ceiling. They pick up sound from a wide area and do not need close proximity to the performer, which does away with the unwanted production of 'popping' and 'booming' sounds, the need for careful positioning in relation to the performer, and the need for microphone technique. In addition, it removes the visual barrier of microphones placed between the performer and the audience. The organisers mentioned that they were particularly concerned about the effect such a physical barrier might have.

Very high-quality speakers had been installed. These were not situated at the front, but some way down the sides of the room, and thus, curiously, only the back two-thirds of the room received sound from the speakers. The organisers explained why this is so:

> *S*: What we've got is sound reinforcement. What I don't like and the artists often won't go for, is a barrage of microphones between them and the audience. What we've got with the microphones in the ceiling – concealed amplification – is that you just get a better sound at the back of the room. You don't have to be right at the front...
> We tend to run every night like this now. Even the floor singers – because they can't see it and they don't have to know how to use microphones.

In addition to the microphones the club had also acquired a sophisticated amplifier and related equipment – for instance, a compressor, pink noise emitter, spectrum analyser and graphic equaliser. The pink noise emitter sends a signal sound out to the speakers which then permits the spectrum analyser to analyse the acoustics of the room. From this the graphic equaliser can then be used to boost certain sound frequency ranges to accommodate for the acoustic properties of the room. The compressor works on the basis that while the overall volume level can be set, there is also an additional volume level which can be modified. Sounds over a given level of volume can be preset to cut out or be scaled down. The compressor is set to scale down sounds over a given volume level by a given ratio, in this case 8:1. The volume of the sound produced over this level would have to rise by a factor of 8 to produce given increases of output volume. And this is not all. In order not to dampen too far sounds which are intentionally loud this equipment has the capacity to build in a 'delay'. The folk club had this set at 5 microseconds. This meant that for a duration of 5 microseconds full volume was emitted before the compressor cut in. This creates an aural hallucination. The full dynamic range is perceived, but ear strain is prevented. The organiser explains:

S: It's just like the whole performing area is live and the way it works is if someone's doing a quiet introduction or a quiet passage of music the whole performing area is live and the whole system's working quite hard and pumping it out, but really nice and clean. Once it gets above a certain level there is a compressor on line which starts cutting the level down. So if people are doing something really loud like a whole band there's hardly anything coming out of the speakers at all.

NLM: Do you mix it?

S: The microphones that are there give virtually a true stereo image.

NLM: What about extraneous noise from the front of the audience?

S: Yes, but the first two or three rows are getting the thing almost totally acoustically anyway and further back they are getting more from the speakers. So there's not a lot of sound at any one time coming out of the speakers, because if someone's doing a quiet passage people are quiet ... so there's nothing for it to pick up apart from the music.

A few points should be made about the use of this equipment in this club. Most significantly, the amplification did not change the framework of the performance. The audience still had to act as if this were an unamplified performance. There was an almost complete absence of any extraneous noise from the equipment – no buzzes, hums or audible distortions of the sound. Another interesting fact concerns the funding of the purchase of the equipment. Several of the folk club musicians had been getting together for a session in a local pub.

S: That went on and it got to a point where on a Tuesday night there was anything up to thirty people playing – a big draw. The pub was packed solid and from there it went on to actually getting some money out of it and it actually went up to £25 a week. And I've kept all that money in a separate account. It wasn't subsidising the club at all because that could have stopped at any time. After eighteen months it was a substantial amount. That's how we've just paid for all the sound reinforcement equipment.

The overall approach to PA by these organisers was initial resistance, followed by scepticism and then acceptance, couched in careful consideration of the way in which technology might restructure the performance. The technology was exploited in such a way as to maintain continuity of the structure of the audience–performer relationship. Such new sound possibilities as the technology made possible were used to reinforce this.

This is, of course, only one club and it is not possible to generalise to the whole of the scene. It is also highly atypical, given that this was the most advanced PA equipment I had come across in any folk club. However, it is relevant to an interpretation of the overall artistic direction of the folk scene in the light of wider musical and social influences and technological possibilities.

These organisers were in fact closer in outlook to the group I had described in the AGM discussion at Aberdeen as the 'antis'. At Chelmsford state-of-the-art equipment had been brought into a folk club, not by those in the vanguard of the introduction of PA into the folk clubs, but by those most distrustful of it. Here is a musical event which has utilised the technological capabilities of modern sound equipment in a highly specialised and particular manner – to enhance the production of acoustic music and to destage.

This has important implications for the future artistic direction of the folk club movement. It can be tentatively suggested that the penetration of electronic sound reproduction may not change the performance ethos of the folk scene. The example of this folk club also indicates that technology, by itself, does not necessarily restructure modes of listening and performing consciousness. The technology itself merely facilitates, and while its development may open up new sound possibilities and new possibilities for structuring musical performances, these should not be viewed deterministically. The restructuring of musical events via the use of PA may have merely set off an ideological struggle within the genre. A folk club which has embraced sophisticated amplification technology is also a club which places great importance on chorus singing, on audience–performer dialogue and on quiet yet informal modes of listening, and seeks to retain its character as a club orientated to the English folk tradition. The fact that it has used innovatory technology to maintain and accentuate these features could be indicative that the spread of PA within the folk scene is not going to lead to the same restructuring of performance which the possibilities opened up by PA and sound technology led to in other musical genres.

13   Conclusion

An editorial in the *Guardian* (7 July 1986, p. 12) referred to the reappearance of 'booing' at London operas, which the writer welcomed as indicating a movement away from the role of opera as 'the aural wallpaper of the rich'. The author argued that if audiences were interested enough and paying enough attention to 'boo' performances which did not meet with their expectations, then this was a healthy development. This is indeed an interesting argument as it stands, but it also speaks volumes about the nature of the writer's underlying conception of an ideal audience–performer relationship. It implies passivity on the part of an 'audience' expecting to be 'entertained' (even if in the cerebral terms of classical musical 'appreciation'). In contrast, I would argue that the almost total absence of booing in the folk scene occurs for reasons quite different to those of modern opera. It certainly is not because within the folk scene all performances are perceived as being of the highest musical standard.

There is something deeper in the direct and inter-communicative form of the audience–performer relationship. The audience survey indicates that a very large proportion of the folk club audience either is, or has been, a performer or organiser. The separation of roles between performer and audience is blurred. As a result, what is communicated in performance and the nature of the performance itself are the embodiment of a quite different set of expectations and interrelationships.

Within the genre there is a striving to return musical performance to the interpersonal level, reducing audience–performer distancing. In these circumstances, to boo would be to boo an act of direct personal communication. Booing is itself a staging device which symbolically reaffirms the existence of a stage and the separation of roles of audience and performer and the one-way nature of communication. If, however, in a subtle way, an audience is expected to contribute something to an event to make it work, then to boo would be to boo oneself. There has been a tendency in several types of musical venue for members of the audience to shout out, just before the commencement of the performance, 'do it'. This is dramatic affirmation of expectations, implying that music is wrapped as presentation, as spectacle, that it is something that is 'done' by some people to others.

The ideology of musical performance affects the nature of the sounds produced. In the folk scene many of the venues are acoustically weak and yet voice production in the manner of Bel Canto has not been adopted. One singer commented to me that when singing high notes in a band she found it hard to resist an attempt to project her voice through the use of a strong vibrato because this was the easiest means of raising the volume of her voice. The singing of folk songs over several other instruments, in fairly large and often acoustically poor venues, exerts a pressure to change vocal techniques, especially those which derive from small intimate settings. However, this singer indicated that to project her voice over the band she had spent a long time practising the production of loud notes of a high pitch without resorting to an operatic style of vibrato, ironically in order to retain what she termed a 'natural voice style'.

The suppression of an ethos of composition also leads to the accentuation of certain features of the music as against others. Although much of the repertoire is held in common, many singers and musicians display their individuality by the means of these styles of phrasing and application of rhythmic inflexions. The 'recipes' of these forms, though applied in a highly individualistic fashion, are learned and transmitted orally. In the context of an instrumental session, features of individual style are developed which do not render a tune unsuitable for playing by several musicians at once.

Folk performers readily step into and out of the role of performer, and this can even happen during a performance. Most performers step into and out of the 'performer' role at the event, even if not while actually performing; getting drinks at the bar which everyone else uses, sitting in the audience when not playing. In discussion with members of the audience on certain occasions I noticed that adverse comments on the evening were mixed with others praising the quality of the performance. A common comment was that somehow the performer had not 'communicated'. I began to notice that this divergence of views might not, to any great degree, indicate a divergence of musical taste, but was a reaction to the degree to which that performer introduced elements of staging into the performance, and whether the members of the audience concerned were socialised into the performing dynamics of the folk scene.

The discouragement of exaggerated movement in performance on stage is further evidence of the rejection of the tendency to transmute the nature of the event into spectacle, to heighten attention to the performer over and above the song. The depression of affectations towards egotistical performance presentation is strong. Particular attention to musical virtuosity can sometimes be paid but this, significantly, is usually accompanied by some form of debunking.

The folk scene is full of counter-elitist strategies which are chiefly targeted on those who are seeking to use positions of power such as top performers and music promoters. The ideals of participation and musical accessibility are not built around simplicity of form. The music is performed within structures which celebrate the fact that 'anybody can do it' but which simultaneously mask minutiae of expression, rhythmic inflexion, decoration and style. A key feature is the development of personal style within regional dialect forms. Like such variations in discourse they are hard to mimic for the same reason that each style derives from and is embedded in a culture.

While I disagree with evolutionary or elitist theories of music, I would stress that different musics in performance do articulate different constellations of meanings and values. Whereas some writers can be quite brazen about the relative superiority of a certain type of music, others can wrap up hierarchical views of music by pointing to a specific sonic feature that a particular musical form has not extrapolated to the same degree as another, and thereby, by implication, point to its inherent inferiority. Thus Etzkorn (1981) argues for the superiority of classical music because the lesser elaboration of tonal and chordal interrelationships by 'vernacular' music compared to 'serious' music renders it more primitive. This is completely to misunderstand the nature of musical meaning. The development of tonal relationships may be the essence of what he terms 'serious' (what I term 'classical') music. But only if music is constructed to celebrate and accentuate tonal relationships – if the meanings through which the music is interpreted are in terms of its tonal relationships – then and only then can the music be interpreted primarily in terms of tonal relationships. To conclude that music whose tonal relationships are simpler is therefore a more simple musical form is quite wrong if that music has accentuated and developed other sonic features through which structures of meaning are communicated.

In folk music some of the sound elements discussed above have become accentuated and elaborated to a high degree. There are, however, many forms of the organisation of the music which could confuse an analyst, not the least of which is the presence of a variety of standards, even at 'mainline' events. At one singing session I happened to be recording and someone came up to me and jokingly said, 'I don't think I'd want that noise in stereo', and I should hasten to add this was a lover of folk music who, as far as I could tell, was also enjoying this rendition.

It was not as if in such instances folk musicians were saying to themselves, 'Ah, but this music is good really'. There is an important feature embedded here. Folk audiences and musicians may recognise that a performance is inadequate according to certain criteria and yet claim that the singer or musician 'had something' or was able to 'put the song over'. Sometimes that 'something' may be held on a high pedestal and on several occasions I was told to ignore the fact that someone had a poor voice or delivery but to listen to their style, or to the effect that they had 'entered' the story of the song. Many disparaging comments are also frequently made about performers whose tone, technique or arrangements of material may be of the highest order but who have not got style, or who come over as insincere with regard to song or tune presentation. It would be ridiculous to judge this music on tonal quality or tonal relationships alone, if a dominant structuring ethos within the genre is the celebration of conviviality, direct human communication, the suppression of inaccessibility through ideologies of 'practising' and excellence, or the telling of a story.

In addition, we cannot understand the nature of what is sonically communicated without reference to its articulation in performance, in actual performances and paying attention to the construction of those performances. This 'construction' should not only be understood physically – stage layout, lighting and so on – but also incorporates the identity of adherents, musically oriented behaviour and the underlying values and meanings which are being expressed and articulated through music within those performances. This is one reason why part of the key to understanding musical performance must be to have an awareness of the social identity of those taking part.

The audience survey has painted a picture of a very specific type of individual, of a very specific habitus (Bourdieu 1984) associated with participation in folk music. The folk scene appeals to those in higher socio-economic class locations, not those who have failed according to the dominant bourgeois materialist ethic. It appeals to those who outwardly conform to the dominant value system, yet who inwardly do not fully identify with this lifestyle. Its referents are taken from the cultural forms of 'lower' socio-economic groups, and one possible explanation could be that these people do not feel comfortable in their new social location. The audience survey has indicated that they are very largely upwardly socially mobile. It is the music of the newly arrived middle classes. Folk music may epitomise or signify a lost world, a sense of community belonging, or nostalgic associations deriving from their personal and family backgrounds in other class locations.

Here, therefore, is an interesting example of upward social mobility associated with 'downward' artistic affiliation. Very different from this would be the upwardly socially mobile aspiring to high culture. My view is that the folk scene attracts those who have benefited materially from upward social mobility, but who have not chosen to identify with and refuse to aspire to the dominant competitive individualistic ethic. A pointer to this is to note that it is a specific sub-section of the middle class which is heavily over-represented in folk music, those in service occupations which are largely in the public sector, jobs such as teaching and social work.

The class location of folkies could be a pointer to the organisational forms of the folk scene and its persistence as a genre. Throughout this study I have mentioned that many features of the socio-musical ideology of the folk revival can also be seen in mid-1970s punk, but the audience survey points to a major difference concerning the distinctive habitus of folkies and punks.

The folk scene may be much more coherently organised than punk, precisely because folkies comprise those who are 'successfully' socialised into our society. Here lies a great irony. Like punks and hippies, folkies celebrate informality, spontaneity and individuality but their organisational structures are highly organised through formal committees and such like. Folkies are people who are inclined to organise. Their involvement in folk music is not a protest about bureaucratic rationality *per se*. 'Middle-class skills' are used to structure and bolster the organisational forms of the folk scene, and it is ironic that a genre which appears to celebrate the counter-bureaucratic ethic of non-hierarchy, participation and communal forms of music-making independent of its commodification, depends on precisely those skills deriving from a middle-class class location. This has a fundamental effect on the trajectory of the scene.

Folk music is not the music of those who have rejected contemporary Western society, but it is a statement by, and for, a certain section of those who have succeeded within it but are not happy to conform to the dominant modes of musical socialisation. However, folk music is not simply a cultural statement. A conspicuous feature of folk music is that its dominant organisational forms – the folk clubs and festivals – are not capitalist forms of organisation. They are not run for profit and are run by the adherents in a bureaucratic/rational manner through committees, networks of organisers, annual general meetings and so on. The folk scene has organised to survive.

Though the folk scene does operate through the medium of the cash nexus it depends on live musical performance. It has resisted adaptation into spectacle and the creation of short-lived stars who enjoy a mass following. It resists popularity. The mechanisms by which the folk scene does this may earn it wide scorn, but these should be seen as an ideological apparatus. Where individuals do 'make it' and become genuinely popular it is not simply that they leave the folk scene: to a certain degree the folk scene leaves them. Several bands which have made the 'cross-over' into wider popularity from the folk scene have reported that they have come across considerable difficulties in remaining within the folk scene, even where they have wished to.

The folk scene, in terms of its presentation, is not concerned with social protest – its message is not directed outwards. It is directed at satisfying the needs of its participants, and its organisational forms permit the celebration of those socio-musical values which dispose towards continuity and permanence. Thus the original folk clubs are now celebrating their thirtieth birthdays – the folk scene is maturing as an entity. The folk scene could even be understood to have itself passed through the same social trajectory as that followed by its adherents. A great many folkies were upwardly mobile during the 1960s and 1970s. The folk scene might have started off as a youth sub-culture in resistance to the commercialisation of music, with a large input of working-class young people, but it is now very much a middle-class and young middle-aged genre. A large element of its support comes from those same people who were drawn into folk music in the 1960s.

The folk scene seems tenacious. It is interesting to speculate in which directions it is heading in the future. Will the professional folk performers cause the professionalisation of the folk scene? Use of PA is spreading widely. There are many consummately skilled performers, but they still have to perform on the same stage as the floor singers. Will this remain so? Will the floor singers gradually vanish? Will the folk scene start to 'polish' its events and try to present them in more 'popular' presentational terms? Will folk music as commodity (re-)emerge? For instance, will recorded folk music start to assume dominance over its live manifestation, as sophisticated recording techniques are taken up by folk performers? Will profit-making folk events emerge? Will a range of intermediate professionals, beyond the small number of agents who exist at present, interpose themselves between folk audiences and folk performers?

There are many indicators that the folk scene has developed within itself mechanisms to maintain its dominant socio-musical ideology in the face of countervailing trends. To give an example, I have mentioned that it is difficult for new performers to become widely known rapidly on the folk scene. Many folk artists pay great attention to publicity and it might be thought that the folk scene could be on the verge of the development of the 'hyping' of newer artists and the 'pushing' of promotional material at folk club booking secretaries. However, a clear demonstration of resistance to this trend became apparent from an institution which has become established recently at one of the two most important English folk festivals, at Whitby in Yorkshire.

This festival is held for a week and takes over the whole town. For the last few years a concert known as the 'Hiring Fair' has been held. Relatively unknown performers are given a platform with very short performing spots, but this should not be understood as a concert in any conventional sense. The concert is attended by large numbers of folk club and folk festival bookings secretaries, who are thereby enabled to hear the new talent which is becoming available on the folk scene. It is literally a hiring fair. As an institution the Hiring Fair has become more and more popular, lasting for several hours and even being held over two days. It can be seen as a mechanism to resist established (in popular terms) pathways by which performers become known. It resists promotion, public relations and packaging. It brings buyer and seller directly together. It is very interesting that this mechanism should have evolved and points to bookings' secretaries, and hence clubs and festivals themselves, seeking to retain direct control.

Part of the scorn which folk music attracts may be because it constitutes a threat. It has taken music whose commonest representation in modern Western society is now as commodity, but it has to some degree removed it from the realm of commodities. Although the cash nexus brings performer and audience together, the events are not run for profit. Furthermore, many performers at these events are not paid and the organisers receive no fee. Within the folk scene there are also many musical events which are not mediated by any financial transaction whatsoever, such as sessions and singarounds. The folk scene is thus a genre which encourages people to produce their own music rather than buy and consume it – in some cases removing the musical form from the cash nexus and the status of commodity altogether. This may constitute a (small) challenge to bourgeois values but not in an overt way. Not surprisingly there are many countervailing tendencies within the folk scene; pressures to reverse this and to change the underlying nature of the folk scene – to turn it into spectacle, to make it 'popular', to remove 'amateurism'.

The resistance to PA cannot be understood merely as resistance to innovation itself, but must be seen as relating more fundamentally to the transmutation of social dynamics. The way in which some folk clubs are now beginning to use PA indicates that, far from resisting new technology in musical production, the folk scene may be tailoring it to its own requirements, applying a high-technology solution in order to attain high-fidelity 'acoustic amplified' sound. It is scarcely surprising that any new technology will be fully explored and exploited by some social group or other. As Bennett (1980) and Frith (1983) indicate, the electronic mediation of musical production is central to and constitutive of the meaning of rock music. Rock music could not exist without it. The forms of rock music performance and of rock music recording depend upon electronic mediation, and rock musicians have accordingly explored the potentialities of developments of electronic sound technology.

However, other musical sub-cultures such as the folk scene appear to have resisted the creative utilisation of sound technology. While they may have used it in some forms, for instance to record an LP, electronic mediation is not used to reconstitute the nature of the musical form, its events and the constituents of musical meaning. This could be understood as straightforward resistance, but this could be a simplistic explanation. It is scarcely surprising that rock music, a musical form which in itself celebrates the potentialities of electronic sound and whose meaning is constituted by it, will be in the vanguard of exploiting the latest sound resources. But the enjoyment of electronically mediated sound in rock music relies not only upon appreciation of the sounds in and for themselves. It relies also on newness: that these are sounds which were not and could not have been produced before. It is this push towards innovation in sound which is essentially, though of course only partially, constitutive of meaning in rock music.

Here lies a major difference between rock music, a musical system which itself evolved through the medium of modern electronic equipment, and other musical forms which largely existed prior to electronic sound reproduction. It is the latter which have been slower to exploit the potentialities of electronic sound. However, in terms of the hypothesis I am going to put forward it would be wrong to see this in terms of resistance.

One of the reasons for the extraordinary success of rock music is that its ideological attachment to 'newness' means that it could readily utilise new sound potentialities and use this to restructure musical communication, in essence rock music evolving through and via the development of sound technology. However, just as this 'newness' can be equated with 'that which is modern and fresh', so this contains within it an essential periodicity. The symbolic function of electronic sound as an emblem of modernity has already waned and as it loses this connotation, when the musical meaning of electronic sound does not mean the negation of other forms of musical communication, then I suspect that we will see the integration of the potentialities of electronic music-making within other genres. I believe this is true of the folk scene today and, in consequence, we may even see a 'reverse newness'. Live, informal, unmediated, acoustic musical production may come to have an aura of freshness and newness, what I would term 'postmodernistic novelty'.

This may in part account for the continued existence of the folk revival and, if so, may herald a promising musical future. The reader may be surprised at this sudden introduction of such a value-laden term as 'promising', but I will readily admit to underlying dispositions which caused me to undertake this project in the first place. I view musical communication as something that ought to be fundamentally interpersonal, yet music has become a commodity: for most people it has ceased to be an active medium of communication. It is something which is consumed, and through this transposition it has ceased to be part of the vernacular realm. This causes me dismay, for the reason that it has resulted in a social disempowerment. People in general now no longer directly communicate through a medium that was once a readily accessible element of social discourse – music. This medium, being one of the most basic and expressive modes of communication – communicative of emotion, mood, identity and culture – is to a large extent produced for some people by others via commodity relations. For most music which is heard in the West there is not a live musician in the vicinity. When one goes to the toilet in a posh hotel and hears soft background music one does not look around for a musician hiding in a cubicle. The resulting depersonalisation, which is generally accepted without question, could be seen as a salutary statement on modern social interaction. The emasculation of the social in music offends my democratic sensibilities. But I see some hope if the 'postmodernistic novelty' thesis stands. If it does, when the novelty of modern sound potentialities wanes in modern music, when 'newness' is no longer partially constitutive of the meaning of these sounds, then the sound resources will come to be used for their merits as sound resources. As such, electronic music may eventually become just another sound resource stripped of the semantic load of modernity. In the process I look forward to a democratisation of musical production, and a return of more musical production to the vernacular domain.

General developments in music must be understood within broader cultural shifts. Stylistic changes occur so fast that little 'new' remains new for long. The oppositional form of punk could be looked at in this way. It pushed an affront to establishment and middle-class values to the limit, but punk characteristics can now even be regarded as respectable. From the historical perspective of a mere fifteen years it is remarkable that punk should not be looked at as something new and shocking and can even be taken as symbolising the *ancien régime*. If symbols of protest and shock value are taken to their extreme and are then diffused through their acceptance as commercial fashion, they are then stripped of their symbolic power to shock and outrage and can even be incorporated into bourgeois values. No longer can the limits of outrage or shock be pushed any further.

As affront and shock value were pushed to their limit in punk they neutered the concept of intentional affront in visual representation and musical performance. It is not simply the form that that affront took in punk – 'gobbing' at audiences or the bodily insertion of safety-pins, for example – but it is the very ability to affront, to shock or to make an overtly confrontational statement that has been muted. In this wider context I thus expect new potent forms of cultural opposition to consumer society to be taken up by oppositional groups which do not claim to affront or shock but which organise within themselves mechanisms for subverting dominant modes of cultural production. Does the folk scene fit into such a model?

A whole range of ethnic revivals are currently being sparked off by the search for identity in the face of international consumer culture. There are now many resurgencies of interest in the cultivation of specifically local forms of popular music, many of which are even being cultivated by the music industry in 'small countries' (Wallis and Malm 1984). The folk scene may be a part of this international trend, comprising an ethnic revival in which its association with cultural forms from the past has been taken up because of an ethnic cultural identification which is specifically English (and Scottish, Yorkshire, Norfolk, and so on).

But it is important to consider the form as well as the content of the artistic 'products' of this revival. The glove as against the bladder is an important cultural statement, as is the search for elements of the style of performance of source traditional music in the context of the folk revival. Folk music has been transported to new social locations but it is important to realise that the very appeal of this music to the revivalists has led to more than the 'surface structures' (Blacking 1971) of the music being transported.

> The surface relations between tones which can be perceived as 'sonic objects' are only part of the deeper systems of relationships which can be described when music is regarded as humanly organised sound.
>
> (Blacking 1971: 93)

And it is the case that many of the 'deep structures' (Blacking 1971) of this music in a traditional setting have been re-created; re-created in the literal sense of a re-creation of extant social meanings. Thus we see the point of such attention to 'authentic' song style in such contrast to the wrapping in 'evening dress' which characterised the folk revival at the turn of the century.

We see elements which have been transmitted over and beyond specific song texts and melodies. The surface structures of the music of the revival have been imbued with a profound social significance derived from their origins as music which was orally created, moulded and transmitted, a music whose function was and is to celebrate community and social solidarity. It is in this way that a common identity of surface structure can evolve, not coincidentally, but deriving from the same deep structures. The folk scene seeks to celebrate continuity and participation, itself a protest against musical passivity, spectacle and commodity. As a form of protest it marks itself off quite differently to punk, where the protest against the ephemeral values of commodification have insufficient capability to resist incorporation into capitalist forms of musical production.

This points to a far more political function of the folk music revival. The emphasis upon vernacular musical creation is itself a powerful ideological and political statement, far more than the creation or singing of songs whose lyrics are overtly political. As Blacking (1973: 95) also points out in the context of Venda society, music is political if only 'it involves people in a powerful shared experience within the framework of their cultural experience and thereby makes them more aware of themselves and of their responsibilities to each other'. Blacking argues that Venda performances where two or more players together create rhythms which can in fact be performed by one, are not musical gimmicks but express concepts of 'individuality in community' and of social, spatial and temporal balance. There is a parallel to the session here. Sessions in the folk scene do not merely create different sounds from, say, orchestras but also express a difference of socio-musical ideology. The folk scene 'wraps' itself differently. The concept of 'sound ideal' (Pegg 1984) as an explanation for the coherence of musical genres is insufficient. It is in terms of the 'wrap' of a Venda performance and of a folk scene session that the expression of individuality in ensemble is to be understood as a statement of the autonomy of cultural production, of socio-musical values which in different ways celebrate individuality in community. Most session musicians do not idealise session music as product, in terms of the sounds produced; they will often turn to concert performances of virtuoso folk performers for their sound ideal, but they will gain greater musical satisfaction from participating in a session.

The folk scene in its three decades of evolution has developed into a complex entity. It is a musical genre which celebrates participation, which celebrates continuity with native traditions, which in its song lyrics expresses comment upon contemporary society and which, in its performance, resists commercialism and stardom. This is not to say that commercialism and stardom do not enter into the folk scene, but where they do they are handled in specialised ways, ways which could actually be seen as defining the genre.

The power of success, especially financial success, to dictate the socio-musical direction of the scene, is restricted. It is limited not merely by the fact that this is not a music that is widely popular, but also by the forms of organisation of the scene, by the structures within which folk musicians operate. What is remarkable is that this structure has become relatively stable and it is in the capacity of the scene to manage itself that we should look for explanations as to why the scene has persisted and has not been wiped out as a passing fad.

The folk scene also encompasses a series of contradictions. These could be viewed as a form of equilibrium resulting from competing pressures. Many of the pressures are hidden. Certainly the desire for intimacy and stardom may be the greatest of all contradictions, one which also runs through other musical genres, but it is the way in which the competing pressures are managed within the folk scene which gives it its specific identity as a coherent musical genre.

The folk scene may be a reaction to the changing role of live music in our culture. It is not simply that the folk traditions of modern Britain are largely moribund, but that for large numbers of people in modern Britain it is no longer socially acceptable to sing in public, even at convivial events, except in specially designated, packaged and boxed 'performances'. The folk scene has resisted this trend in a specific way. It is highly atypical of modern Western musical genres.

Attali (1985) points to the central place of music within a general tendency towards commodification, the replacement of elements of the vernacular domain by those of commodity relations. For him, as music becomes packaged, professionalised and its production specialised, the possibility of general participation is correspondingly decreased.

With the extension of the realm of commodities over more and more cultural and physical domains the creation of small reversals which extend the vernacular domain over the commodified become interesting. When this is accomplished by those who have profited materially from modern society then it becomes doubly interesting. Perhaps the folkies have found their niche as the reluctant bourgeois of contemporary popular culture.

Appendix: Folk Club Survey Tabulations

Table 1 Age of folk club attenders and of the population of Great Britain aged 10 years and over

Total sample				Population of Great Britain aged 10 years and over.	
Age	Count	%		%	
10–14	1	0		9	*********
15–19	2	1	*	10	**********
20–24	13	5	*****	8	********
25–29	32	11	***********	8	********
30–34	70	25	************************	9	*********
35–39	63	23	**********************	7	*******
40–44	35	13	*************	7	*******
45–49	25	9	*********	6	******
50–54	13	5	*****	7	*******
55–59	11	4	****	7	*******
60–64	5	2	**	6	******
65–69	6	2	**	6	******
70–74	3	1	*	5	*****
75–79	0	0		3	***
80–84	0	0		2	**
85+	0	0		1	*

Notes: Sample size = 279
No response = 5
* represents 1%
Source for Great Britain data: OPCS (1983b).

Table 2 Age of first attendance at a folk club

Age	Count	%	
0–4	1	0	
5–9	2	1	*
10–14	23	8	********
15–19	109	39	*****************************
20–24	51	18	******************
25–29	26	9	*********
30–34	20	7	*******
35–39	16	6	******
40–44	11	4	****
45–49	7	3	***
50–54	5	2	**
55–59	2	1	*
60–64	3	1	*

Notes: Sample size = 276
No response = 8
* represents 1%

Table 3 Social class*: Registrar General's classification

	Social class	Count	%	
Folk club	I	34	15	********
sample	II	103	47	************************
	III (N)	45	20	**********
	III (M)	35	16	********
	IV	4	2	*
	V	0	0	
Total population	I		6	***
of Great Britain	II		22	***********
(10% sample)	III (N)		12	******
	III (M)		37	******************
	IV		17	*********
	V		6	***

Notes: * Economically active persons over 16 excluding armed forces
Sample size = 221
No response = 63
* represents 2%
Source for Great Britain data: OPCS (1983b Part 2: 63).

Table 4 Socio-economic group* by sex: folk clubs, Great Britain, persons in employment (per cent)

Socio-economic groups	Persons in employment					
	Folk clubs			Great Britain		
	All	Male	Female	All	Male	Female
Professional	15	21	7	4	6	1
Employers and managers	10	11	10	12	16	7
Intermediate non-manual						
" All:	39	30	52	11	8	15
(" SG 5.1)	38	28	51	10	7	14
(" SG 5.2)	2	2	1	1	1	1
Junior non-manual	18	13	28	26	10	39
Skilled manual and own account non-professional	14	21	1	20	38	7
Semi-skilled manual and personal service	3	4	2	20	17	24
Unskilled manual	0	0	0	6	6	7
Base = 100%	221	132	83	2,417,644	1,473,059	944,585

Note: * Excluding inadequately described/not stated occupations (8% of the total) and members of the armed services (1% of the total) because the Registrar General does not apportion these to socio-economic groups
Source for Great Britain data: OPCS (1984).

Table 5 Highest educational qualification attained, folk clubs and Great Britain (per cent)

		Economically active persons aged 25–69 not in full-time education					
		Folk clubs			Great Britain		
	Total sample Folk clubs	All	Men	Women	All	Men	Women
Degree or equivalent	34	35	36	34	8	10	6
Further education below degree level	23	27	23	33	10	10	10
GCE A level or equivalent	18	17	20	13	7	9	4
GCE O level or equivalent	12	10	9	11	15	14	17
CSE grades 2–5, commercial quals.	1	1	0	3	13	13	13
No qualifications	11	10	12	6	46	43	50
Base = 100%	265	206	124	82	16,923	9,856	7,067

Source for Great Britain data: OPCS (1984: 112).

Table 6 Inter-generational social mobility,* those aged
25–49 not in full-time education

	Folk sample		Great Britain	
	n	%	n	%
Upwardly mobile	97	52	2,030	14
Downwardly mobile	9	5	1,951	14
Static	79	43	10,203	72

Note: * Defined as follows:
    Upwardly mobile: Respondent's educational qualification:
    GCE A level or above; father's socio-economic group:
    manual junior non-manual, own account non-professional
    Downwardly mobile: Respondent's educational qualification:
    GCE O level and below; father's socio-economic group:
    professional, employers and managers, intermediate non-
    manual
    Static: Other combinations of respondent's educational
    qualification and father's socio-economic group
Source for Great Britain data: OPCS (1984: 107).

Table 7 Participation in selected activities, previous four weeks (per cent)

Activities	Folk clubs		Great Britain 1983	
	All	Aged 30–44	All	Aged 30–44
Listened to records/tapes	98	98	63	74
Male	98	99	65	73
Female	97	97	62	76
Visited/entertained relatives and friends	91	91	91	93
Male	90	91	90	92
Female	95	91	93	95
Read books	88	87	56	59
Male	89	86	50	52
Female	88	88	61	65
Gone out for a drink	87	87	54	64
Male	86	90	64	72
Female	88	83	46	57
Gone out for a meal	70	68	40	45
Male	65	63	41	43
Female	79	75	40	47
House repairs/DIY	56	57	36	49
Male	65	67	51	64
Female	46	45	24	34

Table 7   *Continued*

Activities	Folk clubs		Great Britain 1983	
	All	*Aged 30–44*	*All*	*Aged 30–44*
Gardening	39	38	44	52
Male	37	36	50	55
Female	43	43	39	50
Been to theatre/opera/ballet	35	34	4	6
Male	28	30	NA	NA
Female	43	40	NA	NA
Visited historic building*	32	32	8	9
Male	30	27	NA	NA
Female	35	40	NA	NA
Games of skill (not sport)	29	31	14	15
Male	26	32	16	18
Female	35	31	12	13
Needlework/knitting	29	26	27	29
Male	8	7	2	2
Female	58	54	48	54
Visited museum/art gallery	25	23	3	4
Male	22	20	NA	NA
Female	30	28	NA	NA
Keep fit/yoga	20	22	3	4
Male	14	16	0	NA
Female	29	32	5	7
Played squash	7	7	3	4
Male	8	9	4	6
Female	4	5	1	2
Played darts	6	4	7	12
Male	7	6	11	13
Female	4	0	4	5
Played tennis	3	4	1	2
Male	3	3	1	2
Female	3	5	0	NA
Played table tennis	2	2	1	2
Male	2	3	2	2
Female	2	5	0	NA
Played golf	2	2	2	2
Male	1	1	4	5
Female	3	5	0	NA
Musical entertainment (other than theatre/opera/ballet)	all by definition		3	NA
Base = 100%				
All	276	164	19,050	4,930
Male	155	94	8,744	2,353
Female	112	65	10,306	2,577

Notes: * The Great Britain data also include historic sites and towns
       NA = Not available
Source for Great Britain data: OPCS (1983a: 286).

Table 8 Replies to: 'Is there anything you do specifically for the purpose of keeping well and healthy?' Folk club sample and Great Britain 1984 (per cent)

	Folk clubs	Great Britain
Physical training	14	17
Games, athletics	12	17
Walking	55	12
Dieting, special foods	14	7
Eat properly	60	5
Work	20	4
Other	27	14
Nothing	12	40
Base = 100%	276	1,000

Source for Great Britain data: Gallup (1984a).

Table 9 Voting intention at a general election

	Folk club sample			Great Britain
	n	%		%
Labour	102	46	Labour	35
Alliance	65	29	Alliance	26
Conservative	37	17	Conservative	36
Green	10	4		
Nationalist	9	4	Other	2
Communist	1	0		
	224	= 100		1,000 = 100

Source for Great Britain data: Gallup (1987).

Table 10 Types of music most often listened to on records/tapes

	n	%
Folk	165	59
Pop/rock	58	21
Classical	29	10
Jazz	6	2
Blues	3	2
Country (and western)	6	2
Other/various	13	5
Base = 100%	280	

Table 11 Replies to 'Tick the box which best describes why you come to the folk club?'

	n	%
I have a deep interest in the music	136	48
I like the music but I am not deeply interested in it	79	28
I come mainly for the entertainment	48	17
I come mainly for the sociability	13	5
I come because it is something to do	0	0
Other reason	7	2
Base = 100%	283	

Table 12 Musical forms considered to 'belong or have their place' in the folk club (percentage of respondents)

Musical type	Has its place	Does not belong	Undecided/no response
Singers from the tradition	98	0	2
Folk bands	97	0	3
Contemporary singer/songwriters	85	3	12
'New wave' folk bands	67	11	23
Music hall	64	23	13
Blues	63	23	13
Political singers	62	21	17
Country and western	38	43	19
'Trad' jazz	27	58	14
1950s and 1960s rock 'n' roll	23	57	20
Classically trained singing	19	57	25
Modern jazz	14	69	17
Modern 'progressive' rock	10	76	13

Base 284 = 100%

Table 13 Attitudes to folk club floor performers: replies to five stated propositions

	n	%
The folk club should ensure much higher standards of performance from floor performers.	8	3
Although the folk club should give every encouragement to people to perform it could do more to encourage floor performers to raise their standards.	31	12
While there is some need to maintain a high standard of floor performers this should be approached carefully and not be over-emphasised	72	28
Variations in standards are healthy, being the only way that new performers can gain experience	117	45
There is nothing wrong with the general standard of floor performers	30	12
Total sample	258	100

References

Adorno, T.W. (1973) *Philosophy of Modern Music*. London, Sheed & Ward Ltd.

Attali, J. (1985) *Noise: The Political Economy of Music*. Manchester, Manchester University Press.

Atterson, A. (1984) Folk music in East Anglia 1984. Submission to East Anglian Arts Association Music Panel.

Banbury, B. (1981) Morris dance in Scotland, *The Morris Dancer*, 11.

Bell, N. (1963) Preaching to the converted, *Sing*, 7(6), 68.

Bennett, H.S. (1980) *On Becoming a Rock Musician*. Amherst, University of Massachusetts Press.

Berger, P. and Luckmann, T. (1971) *The Social Construction of Reality*. Harmondsworth, Penguin.

Blacking, J. (1971) Structuralism in Venda music, *Yearbook of the International Folk Music Council*, 3, 91–108.

Blacking, J. (1973) *How Musical Is Man?* Seattle, University of Washington Press.

Blacking, J. (1987) Coda: making musical sense of the world. In A.L. White (ed.), *Lost in Music: Culture, Style and the Musical Event*, Sociological Review Monograph 34. London, Routledge & Kegan Paul.

Bourdieu, P. (1984) *Distinction: A Social Critique of the Judgement of Taste*. London, Routledge & Kegan Paul.

Cohen, A.P. (1985) *The Symbolic Construction of Community*. London, Tavistock.

Cohen, A.P. (ed.) (1986) *Symbolising Boundaries: Identity and Diversity in British Cultures*. Manchester, Manchester University Press.

Critcher, C. (1971) Football and cultural values. In S. Hall (ed.), *Working Papers in Cultural Studies*. University of Birmingham: Birmingham, Centre for Contemporary Cultural Studies.

Douglas, S. (ed.) (1986) *Scottish Folk Directory*. Scone, Perth, published privately by author.

Dowell, J. (ed.) (1985) *The Folk Directory 1986*. London, English Folk Dance and Song Society.

Dunn, G. (1980) *The Fellowship of Song*. London, Croom Helm.

Etzkorn, P.K. (1981) The practice of formal music in America. In D. Mark (ed.), *Stocktaking of Musical Life*. Vienna, Doblinger.

French, D. (1982) Letter in *The Morris Dancer*, 12.

Frith, S. (1983) *Sound Effects, Youth Leisure and the Politics of Rock 'n' Roll.* London, Constable.

Gallup International Research Institute (1981) *Gallup Cross-National Values Survey.* London, Gallup.

Gallup International Research Institute (1984a) *Gallup Polls*, Report No. 283. London, Gallup.

Gallup International Research Institute (1984b) *Gallup Polls*, Report No. 290. London, Gallup.

Gallup International Research Institute (1986) *Gallup Polls*, Report No. 310. London, Gallup.

Gallup International Research Institute (1987) *Gallup Polls*, Report No. 318. London, Gallup.

Gersh, G. (1959) Editorial in *Jazz Review*, 2(7).

Goddard, J. (1908) *The Rise of Music.* London, William Reeves.

Goffman, E. (1963) *Stigma.* Englewood Cliffs, New Jersey, Prentice Hall.

Goffman, E. (1974) *Frame Analysis: An Essay on the Organisation of Experience.* Harmondsworth, Penguin.

Harker, D. (1980) *One for the Money: Politics and Popular Song.* London, Hutchinson.

Harker, D. (1985) *Fakesong: The Manufacture of British 'Folksong' 1700 to the Present Day.* Milton Keynes, Open University Press.

Harker, D. (1987) The price you pay: an introduction to the life and songs of Laurence Price. In A.L. White (ed.), *Lost in Music: Culture, Style and the Musical Event*, Sociological Review Monograph 34. London, Routledge & Kegan Paul.

Hobsbawm, E. and Terence, R. (eds) (1983) *The Invention of Tradition.* Cambridge, Cambridge University Press.

Hopkins, P. (1977) The homology of music and myth: views of Levi-Strauss on musical structure, *Ethnomusicology*, 21.

Humphries, R. (1985) *For a Bit of Sport: Molly Dancing and Plough Monday, in East Anglia.* R. Humphries, Linton, Cambs.

Laing, D. (1985) *One Chord Wonders: Power and Meaning in Punk Rock.* Milton Keynes, Open University Press.

Laing, D., Dallas, D., Denselow, R. and Shelton, R. (1975) *The Electric Muse: The Story of Folk into Rock.* London, Methuen.

Lang, P.H. (1941) *Music in Western Civilisation.* New York, Norton.

Lee, E. (1970) *Music of the People.* London, Barrie & Jenkins.

Levi-Strauss, C. (1971) *Mythologique IV.* Paris, L'homme nu.

Lloyd, A.L. (1962) Untitled article, *Spin*, 1(6).

Lloyd, A.L. (1967) *Folk Song in England.* London, Lawrence & Wishart.

MacKinnon, N. (1988) Social identity and the nature of the musical event: a sociological consideration of the British folk scene. PhD thesis, University of Aberdeen.

Malinowski, B. (1923) The problem of meaning in primitive languages. In K.C. Ogden and I.A. Richards, *The Meaning of Meaning.* London, Routledge & Kegan Paul.

Mark, D. (ed.) (1981) *Stock-taking of Musical Life.* Vienna, Doblinger.

McEwen, R. (1965) 'Arts in society', *New Society*, 20 May.

Meek, D.E. (1976) Gaelic poets of the Land Agitation, *Transactions of the Gaelic Society of Inverness*, XLIX.

Merriam, A.P. (1964) *The Anthropology of Music.* Evanston, Illinois, Northwestern University Press.

Morris, D. (1967) *The Naked Ape.* London, Corgi.

Mullen, K. (1983) Public house entertainers: a study of a part-time occupation. M.Litt. thesis, University of Aberdeen,

Munro, A. (1984) *The Folk Revival in Scotland.* London, Kahn & Averill.

Munro, B. (1977) The Bothy Ballads, *History Workshop Journal* 4, 184–93.

Nairn, T. (1988) Charles as Everyman, *New Statesman and Society*, 11 November, 7–8.

Nettl, B. (1956) *Music in Primitive Culture*. Cambridge, Massachusetts, Harvard University Press.

Nettl, B. (1983) *The Study of Ethnomusicology: Twenty-Nine Issues and Concepts*. Urbana and Chicago, University of Illinois Press.

Neuhaus, R. (ed.) (1986) *Unsecular America*. Grand Rapids, Michigan, Eerdmans.

Office of Population Censuses and Surveys (OPCS) (1983a) *General Household Survey*. London, HMSO.

Office of Population Censuses and Surveys (OPCS) (1983b) *Census 1981, National Report, Great Britain*, Parts I and II. London, HMSO.

Office of Population Censuses and Surveys (OPCS) (1984) *General Household Survey*. London, HMSO.

Pegg, B. (1969) Rise up Jock and sing a song, *Club Folk*, 2(4), 8–9.

Pegg, C. (1984) Factors affecting the musical choices of audiences in East Suffolk, England, *Popular Music*, 4.

Perris, A. (1985) *Music as Propaganda: Art to Persuade, Art to Control*, Westport, Connecticut, Greenwood Press.

Seeger, C. (1976) *Studies in Musicology 1935–75*, Berkeley and Los Angeles, University of California Press.

Sharp, C. (1907) *English Folk Song: Some Conclusions*. London, Oxford University Press.

Shepherd, J. (1987) Towards a sociology of musical styles. In A.L. White (ed.), *Lost in Music: Culture, Style and the Musical Event*, Sociological Review Monograph 34. London, Routledge & Kegan Paul.

Shepherd, J. and Vulliamy, G. (1983) A comparative sociology of school knowledge, *British Journal of School Education*, 4(1).

Shepherd, J., Virden, P., Vulliamy, G. and Wishart, T. (1977) *Whose Music? A Sociology of Musical Languages*. London, Latimer New Dimensions Ltd.

Small, C. (1977) *Music-Society-Education*. London, John Calder.

Smith, D. (1986) The folk doom of the 80's?? B.A. (Hons) dissertation, Newcastle upon Tyne Polytechnic.

Smith, J.L. (1987) The ethogenics of music performance: a case study of the Glebe Live Music Club, In M. Pickering and T. Green, *Everyday Culture, Popular Song and the Vernacular Milieu*. Milton Keynes, Open University Press.

Stone, R.M. (1982) *Let the Inside be Sweet: The Interpretation of the Musical Event Among the Kpelle of Liberia*. Bloomington, Indiana University Press.

Taylor, R. (1978) *Art: an Enemy of the People*. Hassocks, Sussex, Harvester Press.

Truzzi, M. (1978) Toward a general sociology of the folk, popular and elite arts. *Research in the Sociology of Knowledge: Sciences and Art*, 1, 279–89.

Van Hoof, J. (1962) Facial expressions in higher primates, *Symposium of the Zoological Society of London 8*.

Wallis, R. and Malm, F. (1984) *Big Sounds from Small Peoples: the Music Industry in Small Countries*. London, Constable.

White, A.L. (ed.) (1987) *Lost in Music: Culture, Style and the Musical Event*, Sociological Review Monograph 34. London, Routledge & Kegan Paul.

Williams, R. (1958) *Culture and Society*. London, Chatto & Windus.

Willis, P.E. (1978) *Profane Culture*. London, Routledge & Kegan Paul.

Woods, F. (1979) *Folk Revival: The Rediscovery of a National Music*. Poole, Blandford.

Wright, D.F. (1975) Repertoire construction: a sociological study of the relationships between composer, performer and listener with particular reference to the Scottish National Orchestra. PhD thesis, University of Aberdeen.

Index

STUDYING POPULAR MUSIC

Richard Middleton

As interest in popular music has increased, so the need for better ways of studying it has become more urgent. However useful, most previous work has concentrated on discrete aspects – sociology, musical history, biography. It is Richard Middleton's contention that popular music can be properly understood only through an interdisciplinary method, and *Studying Popular Music* demonstrates this through a critical analysis of issues and approaches in a variety of areas, ranging from the political economy of popular music through its history and ethnography to its semiology, aesthetics and ideology. It aims to introduce students to the most important literature and theories, and to stimulate scholars and lovers of the music to further research.

The focus of the book is on Anglo-American popular music of the last two hundred years, more especially of the twentieth century. The author argues that this repertory must be located within the musical field as a whole. In Part one, drawing on a dialectical conception of musical development, genre and meaning, he outlines a 'historical map' of this field, offering on the way a constructive critique of existing musical histories, of T.W. Adorno's pessimistic picture of music in twentieth-century 'mass culture', and of various theories of musical production and reproduction in contemporary capitalist societies. Part two turns to the analysis of popular music, looking in turn at approaches drawn from musicology, from folkloristics, anthropology and cultural studies, from structuralism and semiology, and from aesthetics, ideological analysis and psychoanalysis. Throughout the book the elusive character of 'popularity' itself is a constant theme, as it impinges on folk song and music hall, Tin Pan Alley and rock 'n' roll, punk rock and disco, and now 'roots' music. As Constant Lambert and Noel Coward between them observed, the 'appalling popularity' of music gives it an 'extraordinary potency'. To grasp both the 'popularity' of popular music and the 'musicality' of the processes through which this effect is produced requires a cultural theory of music which will undermine existing conceptions of music and musicology; at the same time it will provide a 'musicology of culture' as well – notably of our own.

Contents

336pp   0 335 15275 9 (Paperback)   0 335 15276 7 (Hardback)